Praise for *Creative Thinking in Sch*

In schools we often know why something matters and what we should do about it. But when it comes to teaching creativity, we are less sure about when and how this can best be accomplished. This playbook clearly and thoughtfully translates cutting-edge research into practical creative leadership strategies that will make sustainable change accessible to leaders in schools.

Michael Anderson, Professor of Arts and Creativity Education and Co-Director of CREATE, University of Sydney

All children and young people should have the opportunity to express and channel their creativity throughout their schooling. Any practical resources – such as this exciting new playbook – that can help school leaders and teachers in enabling this to happen are to be warmly welcomed.

Sally Bacon, OBE, Co-Chair, Cultural Learning Alliance and co-author of *The Arts in Schools: Foundations for the Future*

Never was there a greater need for brave leadership to preserve and promote empowering creativity across the curriculum, as an entitlement for every child from every background. So now, in the age of the robots, let's celebrate and teach the habits and discipline of creative thinking and of creative working. This excellent playbook will support courageous school leaders to put creative thinking back at the heart of education where it belongs.

Geoff Barton, General Secretary, Association of School and College Leaders

Creative Thinking in Schools: A Leadership Playbook serves as a roadmap to a series of experiences that leaders can use to reinvigorate their own creative muscles and those of their communities. The playbook includes activities designed to help leaders lead crucial conversations on the role creativity should play in their community as well as structures and facilitation guides that will support them in inculcating creativity into their classrooms, learning environments and communities. For school leaders looking to move the needle, embrace and lead change, this playbook will quickly become your go-to guide for leading professional development and designing the learning environment our students most desperately need and deserve.

Professor Laura McBain, Co-Interim Managing Director, Hasso Plattner Institute of Design, Stanford University

A superb resource for school leaders who wish to support and challenge their teams through active engagement. A unique blend of evidence and activities that promote creativity in action. This is definitely for schools that want to think differently about professional learning.

Dr Simon Camby, Group Chief Education Officer, Cognita Schools

The four purposes of Curriculum for Wales are the shared aspiration for every young person. They provide the opportunity for innovative systems, tools and creative thinking in the education system to create a better future. This playbook provides a practical resource and complements the Creative Leadership Programme that has been recognised and endorsed by the National Academy for Educational Leadership Wales as meeting the needs of leaders in Wales.

Tegwen Ellis, Chief Executive, National Academy for Educational Leadership Wales

This is an outstanding resource, founded on deep knowledge and bursting with provocative ideas and playful strategies for making teaching and leading more creative in your school. Here, seven great experts in creativity, professional learning, leadership and change, give you every reason for, and no excuse for not, livening up your staffrooms, classrooms and online meetings so that they are more creative in their processes and results. In the playbook's own words, it will advance 'creative thinking in all aspects of your school's life'.

Professor Andy Hargreaves, Co-Director, Canadian Playful Schools Network, University of Ottawa

The authors of this magnificent playbook have created something truly amazing – a highly useable and practical resource for leaders. You will be able to transform your school, your network and your jurisdiction. We cannot wait to provide every network school with this book.

Dr Linda Kaser and Dr Judy Halbert, Networks of Inquiry and Indigenous Education, British Columbia

Curriculum for Wales is designed with four core purposes. One of these highlights the importance of creativity; supporting learners to become enterprising, creative contributors, ready to play a full part in life and work. If our learners are to become independent, creative, critical thinkers, then we need to support our school leaders to develop and enhance their skills as independent, creative, critical thinkers too.

This playbook is a wonderful resource that will further enhance and enrich the creative learning programme in Wales, inspiring and supporting leaders to explore new approaches to teaching and learning with creativity at its heart.

Diane Hebb, Director of Arts Engagement, Arts Council of Wales

This wonderful playbook captures the expertise, provocations, lessons learned and insights that a generous community of creative learning experts, researchers, educators and school leaders around the world have shared. Providing a wealth of practical activities and examples in words, diagrams and images, it is a vital resource for any school leader who wants to inspire and coach their team to embed and deliver creative learning strategies across their school.

Tabitha McMullan, Chief Executive Officer, FORM: Building a State of Creativity, Australia

In our ever-changing world, developing creative thinking is essential to help our young people thrive, not only in lessons but also through life. For those leaders with the ambition to build a learning organisation with creativity and achievement for all at its heart, this playbook brings a fantastic collection of information, ideas and practical resources to do just that. It's a must for those with a wider view of education today.

Andy Moor, Chief Executive Officer, Holy Family Catholic Multi Academy Trust

This playbook has universal appeal across countries. It provides insightful tools for school communities to develop creative thinking, unlocking potential and hidden leadership from everyone in schools. The playbook's universal usability also makes it a perfect gift for anyone in the international community of creative thinking in schools.

Dr Kraiyos Patrawart, Managing Director, Equitable Education Fund, Thailand

The playbook deliberately places emphasis on the creative dimension of leadership, becoming comfortable with openness, offering greater trust, developing spaces for new thinking. I highly recommend it.

Dame Professor Alison Peacock, Chief Executive Officer, Chartered College of Teaching

We know that creative thinking is critical for our young people – but too often, our curricula and cultures don't nurture these skills. This playbook gives practical tools to support all leaders to consider why this work is so important, and how to make it happen.

Liz Robinson, Chief Executive Officer, Big Education Multi-Academy Trust

I particularly like the way in which the playbook is both soundly rooted in research and also enjoyably creative and playful in the approach to professional learning.

Andreas Schleicher, Director for Education and Skills, Organisation for Economic Co-operation and Development

This leadership playbook is a really valuable resource for school leaders who want to cultivate the creativity of their students in all subjects by developing the confidence and skills of their staff. It very much mirrors the learning emerging from the eight pilot Creativity Collaboratives across England where early results suggest that teaching for creativity is a welcome and attainable goal for all schools.

Sir Nicholas Serota, Chair, Arts Council England

This playbook is an essential resource for anyone who cares about the place of creativity in education, providing accessible yet expert guidance to nurture and sustain creative thinking, creative teaching and creative learning.

Mags Walsh, Programme Director, Scoileanna Ildánacha/Creative Schools, Ireland

This playbook aligns with the key focus of the Curriculum for Wales on supporting creativity, as one of the skills integral to its four purposes. It will be a valuable resource to help school leaders develop their talents and skills.

Welsh Government Education Directorate

CREATIVE THINKING IN SCHOOLS

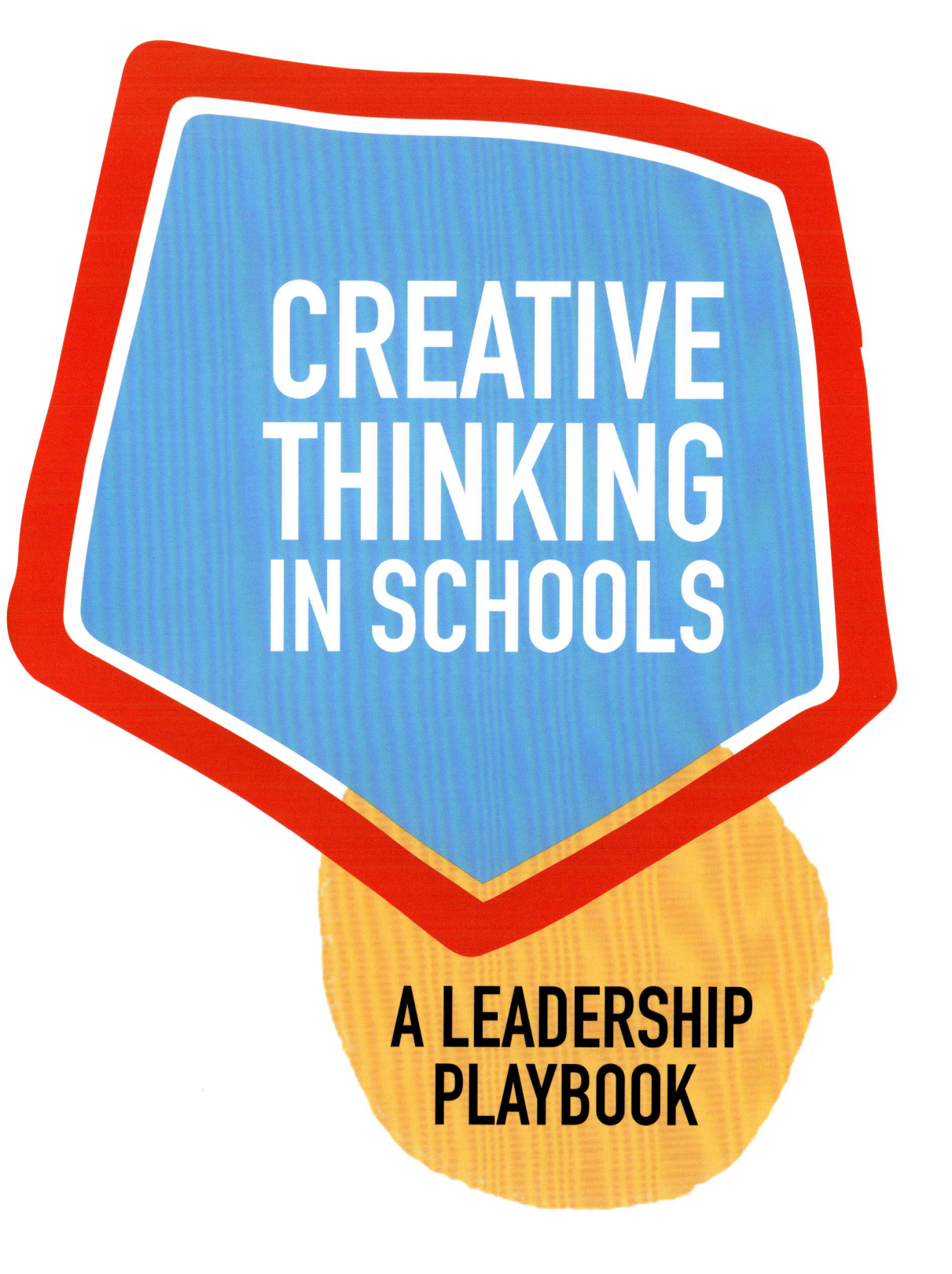

A LEADERSHIP PLAYBOOK

Bill Lucas, Ellen Spencer, Louise Stoll, Di Fisher-Naylor, Nia Richards, Sian James and Katy Milne

Crown House Publishing Limited
www.crownhouse.co.uk

First published by

Crown House Publishing Ltd
Crown Buildings, Bancyfelin, Carmarthen, Wales, SA33 5ND, UK
www.crownhouse.co.uk

and

Crown House Publishing Company LLC
PO Box 2223
Williston, VT 05495, USA

www.crownhousepublishing.com

© Bill Lucas, Ellen Spencer, Louise Stoll, Di Fisher-Naylor, Nia Richards, Sian James and Katy Milne 2023

The right of Bill Lucas, Ellen Spencer, Louise Stoll, Di Fisher-Naylor, Nia Richards, Sian James and Katy Milne to be identified as the authors of this work has been asserted by them in accordance with the Copyright, Designs and Patents Act 1988.

Icons and artwork © Creativity, Culture and Education, 2022.

Page 140: images unsplash.com.

All rights reserved. Except as permitted under current legislation no part of this work may be photocopied, stored in a retrieval system, published, performed in public, adapted, broadcast, transmitted, recorded or reproduced in any form or by any means, without the prior permission of the copyright owners. Enquiries should be addressed to Crown House Publishing Limited.

Crown House Publishing has no responsibility for the persistence or accuracy of URLs for external or third-party websites referred to in this publication, and does not guarantee that any content on such websites is, or will remain, accurate or appropriate.

British Library of Cataloguing-in-Publication Data
A catalogue entry for this book is available from the British Library.

Print ISBN: 978-178583684-8
Mobi ISBN: 978-178583685-5
ePub ISBN: 978-178583686-2
ePDF ISBN: 978-178583687-9

LCCN 2023933210

Printed in the UK by
Gomer Press, Llandysul, Ceredigion

Foreword by Andreas Schleicher

In a world in which the things that are easy to teach and test have also become easy to digitise and automate, the capacity of individuals to imagine, create and build things of intrinsic worth is rising in importance. Schools today need to prepare pupils for a period of extraordinarily rapid economic and social change, for jobs that haven't yet been created, to use technologies that haven't yet been invented and to solve social problems that we can't yet imagine. People need to be able to imagine new solutions, connect the dots between things that previously seemed unconnected, see new possibilities and turn them into new products or ways of living.

All this makes creative thinking vital. And it presents a particular challenge to school leaders who need to inspire their teachers to ensure that their pupils achieve the best qualifications they can in whatever accountability regime they find themselves, but also to prepare their pupils for uncertain, challenging times.

In 2022, for the first time, the Organisation for Economic Co-operation and Development's (OECD) Programme for International Assessment tested the creative thinking of 15-year-old pupils in an international comparative setting. In selecting creative thinking as the focus of its new test, the OECD is explicitly seeking to raise the status of this important human competence. When we publish the results of this groundbreaking test, I hope it will act as a spur to policymakers, leaders and teachers to embed creative thinking in every aspect of school life.

The Creative Thinking test, along with other advances in our understanding led by my colleagues at the OECD's Centre for Educational Research and Innovation and by Professor Bill Lucas and his research team, provides an opportunity for school leaders across the world to make a step change in their practices. We increasingly know about curriculum design, the selection of signature pedagogies and how best to evidence the progress of young people's creative thinking skills, but for real change to happen we need to focus on building the knowledge, confidence and capabilities of the teaching profession to deliver these changes at scale.

Creative Thinking in Schools: A Leadership Playbook lays out a series of evidence-based activities that school leaders can use with their staff to consider what creativity is, how it can be taught and assessed, and what cultural and system changes need to be put in place to enable this to happen. I particularly like the way in which the playbook is both soundly rooted in research and also enjoyably creative and playful in the approach to professional learning that it offers.

Andreas Schleicher, Director for Education and Skills, and Special Advisor on Education Policy to the Secretary-General at the Organisation for Economic Co-operation and Development

Foreword by Professor Dame Alison Peacock

Creativity has been lazily maligned by some influential educationalists for too long. The theory goes that children cannot be given space to imagine, to develop criticality or to think for themselves as this is inefficient compared with direct instruction. On the contrary, we need children critically to appraise the knowledge they are taught, learn to play with big ideas, forge connections and make sense of the world. These skills rarely flourish in a siloed curriculum.

By the same token, it has been assumed that creativity is the unique preserve of the arts. It is not. While the arts provide many opportunities to cultivate creativity, you can be creative in any and every aspect of the school curriculum and in the wider community. Scientists need to think creatively to make advances in understanding. Mathematicians need to challenge assumptions and use their imagination to make new connections and see problems with fresh eyes. Creativity is ubiquitous.

This playbook offers a wide range of activities and resources aimed at scaffolding professional creative thinking among teaching colleagues. As core purposes are reviewed, the aim is to free up colleagues, enabling them to develop a tolerance of uncertainty as perceived constraints are diminished. This is not about discarding current approaches to pedagogy, curriculum and assessment. Rather, it's about noticing and responding to the space for creativity across all areas of school life. It's about the use of frameworks such as 'creative habits' to review and further develop whole-school thinking. I particularly like the way in which the authors consider the development not just of pupils' creativity but of the adults who care for them too.

Much has been written about leadership and the skills required to manage change. Usually, such texts focus on 'school improvement' with the core focus on measurable outcomes. In this work, the authors deliberately place an emphasis on the creative dimension of leadership. This means becoming comfortable with openness, offering greater trust and developing spaces for new thinking. To be a creative leader is to be someone who goes beyond traditional leadership towards enabling transformative practice, supporting the development of signature creative pedagogies, embracing diversity and celebrating difference.

Through collaboration and the development of agency, creative leadership energises colleagues, ultimately becoming part of the DNA of a school culture. The professional learning activities in this playbook encourage colleagues to disrupt existing habitual behaviours, to reflect on core purposes and, ultimately, to build a collaborative theory of change. This is about building greater organisational intellectual strength through establishing core threads and patterns which support the curriculum and transform overall standards of achievement.

I recommend this resource to you as the nudge we need to move our profession towards greater consideration of what really matters in education. We want to have it all, but in seeking this we must recognise that a model of schooling that allows a third of our children to be labelled as failures at 16 is a model that needs reform. Embracing creativity, celebrating neurodiversity as strength and embracing a rich talent-filled approach to education means setting up our children to flourish.

Professor Dame Alison Peacock, CEO, Chartered College of Teaching, England

Preface

For nearly two centuries, teachers have focused largely on what has become known as the knowledge contained in the 3Rs – reading, writing and arithmetic. At the macro level, educational jurisdictions – the countries and states that set policy for schools – are upgrading their view of what schools should be teaching and learning. Now, it's time to recognise some of the additional broader skills and dispositions that are needed today – for example, the 3Cs of communication, collaboration and creative thinking.

The focus of this resource, what we're calling a playbook, is on the last of these three, creative thinking. And, as we explore the leadership challenges of embedding creativity in schools, we'll use the metaphor of plays in this playbook, as we help school leaders to play the game of learning in ways that will transform the lives of their pupils and staff.

We've reached a global tipping point for creative thinking in schools. Some countries – Australia, Canada, Finland, Ireland, Norway, Scotland and Wales, for example – have embraced the 3Cs wholeheartedly in their national curricula. Countries like these, which see creative thinking as important, tend to think of their curricula not just in terms of individual subjects but also as a set of wider competences which can be embedded in all disciplines. Others, England is one of them, have been resistant, seeing the introduction of creative thinking, for instance, as somehow distracting pupils from the knowledge they need to acquire in specific subjects.

A few of us (the authors) live and/or work in Wales where changes are already happening. Most of us live in England, although have experience of working with many other systems across the world, so we can see the big differences in approaches. After what seems like a very long wait, the landscape for creativity and creative thinking in English schools is becoming more positive. In 2019, the Durham Commission on Creativity and Education published its first report, making clear the importance of creativity and creative thinking in schools.[1] Its major recommendation was that networks of schools willing to make a reality of embedding creative thinking in every aspect of school life should be given significant funding. In 2021, eight Creativity Collaboratives were launched, and this significant investment is driving interest across England.[2]

Mounting evidence internationally of the importance of creative thinking has led to the situation where the challenge to school leaders isn't *whether* to focus on creative thinking but *how*.[3] And, all the while, schools have to be mindful of the political context in which they operate, that current governments have specific issues on which they're focusing, and that inspections of schools can both enhance and undermine brave leaders who are trying to do something different. We know that where a country prioritises creative thinking, schools will find it considerably easier to do the same. But there are things schools can do – and choices they can make – around developing creative thinking to ensure that children and young people can flourish now and in their future, whatever educational system they grow up in. This depends on creative leadership.

Creative leadership is important because creative thinking is important, and all change in schools requires the commitment and active engagement of leaders. There's a multidimensional argument for the importance of creative thinking that includes wellbeing, employability, economic growth, the fast-paced nature of change in the world today, a growing international impetus and the broader educational benefits of creativity.

---

1. Arts Council England and Durham University, *Durham Commission on Creativity and Education* (London: Arts Council England, 2012), p. 3. Available at: https://www.artscouncil.org.uk/sites/default/files/download-file/Durham_Commission_on_Creativity_04112019_0.pdf.
2. See https://www.creativityexchange.org.uk/creativity-collaboratives.
3. B. Lucas, *Creative Thinking in Schools Across the World: A Snapshot of Progress in 2022* (London: Global Institute of Creative Thinking, 2022).

Across the world, many education systems are making progress with fostering creativity within educational settings. We'll draw on these throughout the playbook. That the Programme for International Student Assessment (PISA) test of creativity of 15-year-olds was carried out for the first time in 2022 is a clear indication of a global direction of travel.[4]

The model of creativity and creative thinking that underpins this playbook focuses on five key creative habits of mind – *inquisitive, persistent, collaborative, disciplined* and *imaginative* (see **Resource 1: Five Creative Habits Framework**). There's strong evidence of the value of each one of these habits.

As well as arguments that are essentially about the value of creative thinking, there are also some that are specific to the particular challenge of leading creative thinking in schools today. These include the need to be robustly articulate in challenging five myths which still survive today – that creativity: (1) is too vague to be teachable, (2) is inherited and not learned, (3) is uniquely the preserve of the arts, (4) detracts from a 'standards' agenda and (5) isn't connected with 'domain' knowledge.

We've developed this resource to help you strengthen your creative leadership. It'll provide you with evidence on all these issues and more. We hope that it'll be valuable to you wherever you are and that its approaches to school leadership will be widely transferable across the world.

---

4   Organisation for Economic Co-operation and Development, *PISA 2021: Creative Thinking Framework* (Third Draft) (Paris: OECD, 2019). Available at: https://www.oecd.org/pisa/publications/PISA-2021-creative-thinking-framework.pdf.

Acknowledgements

Thank you to:

The Mercers' Company who funded research into the leadership of creativity in schools undertaken by the Centre for Real-World Learning (CRL) at the University of Winchester and supported the development of the playbook.

The Comino Foundation for its long-term commitment to funding the Centre for Real-World Learning's focus on developing the creative thinking capabilities of all young people.

Creativity, Culture and Education for supporting the original research which led to the development of CRL's Five Creative Habits framework used in the playbook and for funding the development of the playbook.

The Arts Council of Wales for their longstanding commitment to using the CRL framework and for funding an online platform to support the playbook.

The many schools we've partnered with and learned from, including those involved in CRL's research with Mercers, the eight Creativity Collaboratives in England, lead creative schools in Wales, FORM's Creative Schools programme in Western Australia and schools undertaking research into the assessment of creative thinking as part of Rethinking Assessment.

The many creative practitioners and educators whose work has been influential in the development of the plays, including Paul Collard, Paul Gorman, Sophie Hadaway, Sam Holdsworth, Marie Othilie Hundevadt, Greg Klerkx, Sally Pilkington and Lamis Sabra.

We're particularly grateful to Greg Ross and Richard Harrison at the UCL Centre for Educational Leadership, and to Simon Rogers and Laura Morris at Walsall Academy for feedback on draft activities.

Contents

Foreword by Andreas Schleicher i
Foreword by Professor Dame Alison Peacock ii
Preface iii
Acknowledgements v

Introduction 1

Part 1: Warming Up 7

Warm-Up 1: Explore Creativity and Creative Thinking 9
- Activity 1 — Understand the Essence of Creativity 10
- Activity 2 — Find the Creative You 15
- Activity 3 — Explore Creative Habits 17
- Activity 4 — Chart Your Creativity Over Time 19
- Activity 5 — Notice Creativity in Action 21

Warm-Up 2: Shift the Paradigm 23
- Activity 6 — Be Clear About the Purpose of School 24
- Activity 7 — A Different Kind of School 26
- Activity 8 — A Different Kind of Leadership 28
- Activity 9 — Creative Leadership in Action 31

Part 2: Playing the Whole Game of Learning 35

Play 1: The Change Process 37
- Activity 10 — Use a Theory of Change 38
- Activity 11 — Hang Out the Change Plan 40
- Activity 12 — Develop Powerful Networks 42
- Activity 13 — Identify Challenges, Barriers and Uncertainties 44
- Activity 14 — Mitigate Risks 46

Play 2: Develop Leaders 49
- Activity 15 — Identify, Enable and Grow Creative Change Catalysts 50

Play 3: Change the Culture 53
- Activity 16 — Core Values to Support Creativity 54
- Activity 17 — Develop a Common Language 59
- Activity 18 — Debunk Myths About Creativity 62

Play 4: Rethink Structures 65
- Activity 19 — Thread It Through the School Improvement Plan 66
- Activity 20 — Reimagine Systems 67

Play 5: Develop a Creative Curriculum 69
- Activity 21 — Embed Creativity in the Curriculum 70
- Activity 22 — Look Beyond the Classroom 72

Play 6: Rethink Pedagogy 73
- Activity 23 — Use Signature Pedagogies for Creativity 74

Play 7: Track Progression in Creative Thinking 77
- Activity 24 — Rethink Assessment 78
- Activity 25 — Develop Creativity Assessment Literacy Among Staff 80

Play 8: Ensure Professional Learning 83
- Activity 26 — Create Opportunities for Powerful Professional Learning 84

Play 9: Collaborate with External Partners 87
- Activity 27 — Nurture and Learn with External Partners 88
- Activity 28 — Learn with Other Schools 90
- Activity 29 — Foster Creative Mindsets By Looking Outside Education 93

Play 10: Reflect and Evaluate 97
- Activity 30 — Review and Fine-Tune 98

Call to action 101

Resources 103

Resource 1 Five Creative Habits Framework 104
Resource 2 Descriptions of the Creative Habits 105
Resource 3 Creativity Habits Web Template 107
Resource 4 Creative Individuals Are … 108
Resource 5 Curriculum, Pedagogy and Assessment/Progression Venn 113
Resource 6 Schools as Learning Organisations: Stimulating Environments for Creative Thinking 114
Resource 7 School as a Learning Organisation Plan 117
Resource 8 Creative Leadership Plays 119
Resource 9 Creative Leadership Plays – Notes 124
Resource 10 Using a Theory of Change in Schools 126
Resource 11 Intervention Cards 128
Resource 12 Thinking About How Social Networks Can Support Educational Change 133
Resource 13 Common Change Challenges 135
Resource 14 Example Risk Matrix 136
Resource 15 Great Teacher Leader Characteristics 138
Resource 16 The What and Who of Leadership 139
Resource 17 Images for Identifying, Growing and Enabling Change Catalysts 140
Resource 18 What Are You Doing? What Might You Do? 141
Resource 19 Evidence Sheet 142
Resource 20 The Power of Language 143
Resource 21 Five Myths About Creativity 144
Resource 22 Thinking About Your Locality 145
Resource 23 Signature Pedagogies for Creative Thinking 146
Resource 24 Rethinking Assessment Figures 147
Resource 25 A Repertoire of Methods for Assessing Creative Thinking 149
Resource 26 Learning Progression for 'Inquisitive' 150
Resource 27 Pupil Self-Report for 'Inquisitive' 151
Resource 28 Twenty Professional Learning Activity Cards 152
Resource 29 Powerful Professional Learning Grid 157
Resource 30 Peer Learning Prompt Cards 158
Resource 31 The Peer Learning Cycle 159
Resource 32 Richards and Hadaway Reading 160

Bibliography 161
About the authors 164

Introduction

Playbook, *noun*

1. A book containing play scripts.
2. *Sports* A notebook that contains descriptions or diagrams of the plays of a team, especially a football team.
3. A set of tactics often used by people engaged in competitive activities.[1]

Across the world, schools are changing as they increasingly try to 'play' what David Perkins calls the 'whole game' of learning, one in which a broad set of dispositions, skills and knowledge are equally valued.[2] The concept of a playbook comes from American football where teams describe the specific moves or 'plays' that they would put into practice on the field. But the term is also being used to describe how different situations should be addressed by individuals and teams. The *Cambridge Business English Dictionary* defines it as 'a set of rules or suggestions that are considered to be suitable for a particular activity, industry, or job'.[3] Increasingly, it's being used by those developing leadership resources.

We like it because the word 'play' also has the sense of experimentation or, as in the playlists of music many of us create on our phones, it conveys a feeling of emotional attachment to what we've chosen. The drama analogy reminds us that leadership inevitably involves conflict and that there are effective ways of managing this. The 'descriptions and diagrams' in the second definition above speak to our need for clear how-tos and helpful models. And the competition aspect isn't, of course, about the idea of winning a team game but about being seriously tactically successful in improving the life chances of young people and, in particular, their ability to think creatively. Play is also associated with early childhood where young children learn through play, which is both enjoyable and challenging and is scaffolded to extend their development. We explicitly invite you to be playful as you explore creativity in your school.

In this resource, we offer powerful research, professional learning materials and facilitation approaches to enable you, as leaders, to embed creative thinking in all aspects of your school's life, or schools' lives if you're leading a number of schools, while at the same time thriving within whatever accountability regime you're working within. It's aimed at all those who play a leadership role in and around schools, including, for example, multi-academy trust CEOs in England, district and municipal leaders, network leaders, head teachers and principals, senior leaders, middle leaders and other teacher leaders. In this extended group, we include both those with a specific brief for creativity and those who lead continuous professional development and learning more generally. All of the activities are designed for you, but you may want to include others as appropriate or over time.

The playbook draws on two decades of learning by the authors and the school leaders with whom we've worked across the world. We see it as evolving over time, with supporting materials and further activities added to our website.[4] We also know that colleagues involved in Creativity Collaboratives around England, and in similar initiatives across the world, are also developing tools which will provide additional beneficial sources of support.

Research suggests that embedding complex ideas like creativity in complex organisations like schools takes time.[5] Minimally, we imagine schools making a one-year commitment; ideally, three years. In parallel, we see the endeavour as being explicitly part of the school's or network's improvement or development plan. Such an investment of time will also require the allocation of key roles for those who are leading the change.

---

1 See https://www.wordnik.com/words/playbook.
2 D. Perkins, *Making Learning Whole: How Seven Principles of Teaching Can Transform Education* (San Francisco, CA: Jossey-Bass, 2009).
3 R. Combley (ed.), *Cambridge Business English Dictionary* (Cambridge: Cambridge University Press, 2011).
4 See https://www.leadingforcreativethinking.org.
5 T. Burner, Why is Educational Change So Difficult and How Can We Make It More Effective? *Forskning og forandring*, 1(1) (2018): 122–134. https://doi.org/10.23865/fof.v1.1081

We've carefully considered the order of the activities. Many schools may choose to approach the tasks involved in the order they're presented. But, of course, you'll all start from different bases and be guided by different priorities, so we've designed activities that can be used as flexibly as possible. You'll see that there are some short readings with key content that underpin the playbook's orientation to creativity, creative thinking, creative leadership and creative schools. Sometimes it might be important to read these in advance or during a session. Otherwise, we offer all the plays and activities within them as suggestions rather than rules you have to follow, hoping that you'll want to adapt them and develop your own school or community-based playbook.

The playbook is divided into two parts – Part 1: Warming Up and Part 2: Playing the Whole Game of Learning. The warm-ups provide critical ideas and related activities which underpin the creative leadership plays that follow and, we believe, are important in helping you to engage most beneficially in the play activities. The contents list on pages vii–viii will give you a quick overview of the warm-ups and plays.

The remainder of this section introduces you to the playbook and things to think about as a facilitator. Warm-up 1 activities invite you to explore creativity and creative thinking, notice and consider your own creativity and creative thinking, and chart your journey over time. Warm-up 2 activities emphasise the shift in paradigm needed in thinking about the purpose and kind of school in which creativity and creative thinking can thrive, and the different kind of leadership needed.

Part 1 ends with a description of creative leadership in action and introduces the 10 plays that you'll encounter in Part 2 (see the table below). You can find more details in warm-up **Activity 9**). Each play in Part 2 contains one or more activities.

Play number	Creative leadership plays
1	The Change Process: Articulate a clear description of the process of change, so everyone understands how young people's creativity will be developed.
2	Develop Leaders: Identify and nurture creative change catalysts/teacher leaders.
3	Change the Culture: Create a culture in which creativity is promoted and valued in every aspect of the school's life and reflected in the school's improvement plan.
4	Rethink Structures: Build creative thinking into all resourcing.
5	Develop a Creative Curriculum: Embed creativity into a coherent curriculum.
6	Rethink Pedagogy: Develop staff confidence in using teaching and learning methods that cultivate creativity.
7	Track Progression in Creative Thinking: Find ways to assess that explicitly recognise progress in the development of young people's creativity.
8	Ensure Professional Learning: Make creativity a focus of staff professional learning.
9	Collaborate with External Partners: Invest in external partners and funding to help develop creativity.
10	Reflect and Evaluate: Explore, reflect on and evaluate your school's journey to creativity.

An example activity

Each activity clearly shows:

- Its purpose.
- Which of the five creative habits it may help you to develop in yourself because it's important for you to model the creative habits.
- Timings, which are adjustable as appropriate.
- Any resources needed and how to set up the activity, if necessary.
- Guidance for how to get going and carry out the activity.
- Reflection questions for you to use and adapt. We suggest you experiment with different reflection techniques. Scan this QR code for some ideas:

Purpose

Facilitation involves using a range of interactive processes to enable a group of people to learn together. This activity introduces some of the key processes involved and suggests ways in which school leaders can use facilitation as a key element in the change process. The premise is that unless you choose professional learning methods that are genuinely participatory, it's highly unlikely that your colleagues will engage with you and adapt the ways they teach!

This activity might also develop your creative habit of being …

You'll see the following table at the start of every activity. We've filled in the creative sub-habits that we think the activity particularly promotes. You may think of others as you go through the activity. We encourage you to talk about this in the groups that engage in the activities.

Inquisitive sub-habits	Persistent sub-habits	Collaborative sub-habits	Disciplined sub-habits	Imaginative sub-habits

Where a creative habit is less relevant to an activity, its colour is less bright to show this.

Duration

1 hour

The timings are approximations and to be adapted as necessary; the timings in this introduction are just examples. Most activities are between 1 hour and 1 hour 15 minutes. Some are intended to be repeated or returned to over time, and some, such as peer visits (see **Activity 28: Learn with Other Schools**) might take a whole day.

Resources and setting up

As a facilitator, you'll need to have a generic toolbox of helpful resources, and we mention specific resources when they're needed. The numbered resources 1–32 can be found at the back of the playbook. In any activity, you may wish to make **Resource 2: Descriptions of the Creative Habits** or **Resource 4: Creative Individuals Are …** visible to participants to keep the creative habits in mind. You'll want to decide whether you use materials or technological approaches.

Getting going

STEP 1 15 minutes

The voice we've used throughout reflects our belief that all leaders need to learn how to facilitate groups and to be thinking constantly about being proactively interactive with colleagues. So, for example, we might say 'Work in threes to brainstorm possible associations with the word creativity and share these' rather than 'Split the group into threes. Ask them to brainstorm possible associations with creativity and then get them to feed back in turns' and so on. Our assumption is always that we're speaking directly to you as a creative leader engaged in the process of embedding creativity in your school, and that there's a level of confidence in you to turn our direct requests into activities!

In short, facilitators are there to support and enable colleagues' learning. To return to the sporting analogy of a playbook, coaches are essential to success in sport. In sport, as in education, great coaches facilitate learning and develop capacity for change. To get the most from engaging with the activities, it'll help if you think of yourselves as facilitators of your own and others' learning and development.

Try this. Divide an open space into two down the middle using thick masking tape. Explain that one side of the line is 'agree' and the other 'disagree'. Read out the statements below and ask the participants to take a position on one side of the line. After each statement, ask some participants to explain their reason(s) and attempt to persuade those on the other side to change their mind. Participants are free to move sides if they're convinced.

- Facilitating a workshop is the same as chairing a meeting.
- You don't need to be an expert to facilitate a workshop.
- Having no agenda helps a session to be more creative.

- It's fine for facilitators to spend most of the time delivering information.
- The facilitator's opinion isn't important.
- It's the facilitator's job to tell people when to stop talking.
- It's good to take turns in facilitating staff learning sessions.

Did you all agree? Were there some statements for which you wanted to say 'It depends'? As Deirdre Le Fevre and her colleagues in New Zealand remind us, facilitators have an important dual role.[6] They have both agency themselves and develop collective agency in and with others. A good facilitator effectively increases the collective intelligence of any group.

Going deeper

STEP 2 45 minutes

You'll find that the activities in this playbook frequently involve you in dialogue – the kind of talk Louise Stoll calls learning conversations.[7] Such conversations, among other things:

- Are intentional, purposeful, focused and supported by frameworks and guidelines to help participants structure their dialogue and interrogate evidence or ideas.
- Are planned to ensure that everyone feels and is involved through a constructive balance of comfort and challenge.
- Are more fruitful when they involve diverse perspectives and voices, including all of your important stakeholders.
- Benefit from being allocated time and space and use of dialogue skills, such as listening, questioning, challenging, probing, connecting and building on others' ideas.
- Are more productive when they're underpinned by a culture of trust and inquiry, where people engage with curiosity, interrogating words, ideas and each other respectfully.
- Stimulate deep reflection that challenges thinking and assumptions as colleagues make meaning together, jointly coming up with new insights and knowledge.
- Promote intentional change to enhance practice and pupil learning and wellbeing. It's not just talk and no action. Commitment exists that new knowledge and learning will be put to use to benefit pupils and the entire learning community.

Facilitators need to have lots of effective ways of making text come alive. Look at **Activity 6: Be Clear About the Purpose of School**, for example. You'll see that we suggest using a diamond nine process to help you think through different perspectives and then rank them. This makes an activity that might normally be passive and individual more interactive. Another good example of this is jigsaw activities. This is a strategy that encourages people to develop their own understanding and then share their knowledge with a group. Groups are each given a particular part of a problem or text and then come back to share their thoughts, building a fuller picture, like the pieces of a jigsaw.

Try the technique on a reading of your choice. In 'home' groups of three, number yourselves 1, 2 and 3. Each choose a separate reading from the playbook and spend five minutes reading it. Now move to your 'expert' group (people who have been allocated the same reading as you). In this group consider:

- What the reading tells you about creativity, creative thinking, creative leadership and/or schools that nourish creativity.
- What the key points are in this reading that you want to convey to your home group.

---

6 D. Le Fevre, H. Timperley, H. Twyford and F. Ell, *Leading Powerful Professional Learning: Responding to Complexity with Adaptive Expertise* (Thousand Oaks, CA: Corwin Press, 2020).
7 L. Stoll, Stimulating Learning Conversations. *Professional Development Today*, 14(4) (2012): 6–12.

In your home group, take it in turns to share your readings with each other, then reflect on the following:

- What these readings together tell you about creativity, creative thinking, creative leadership and/or schools that nourish creativity.
- Whether your readings have added to your thinking about developing creativity in your school/across your schools and, if so, in what ways.

Reflecting together

STEP 3 15 minutes

Throughout the playbook you'll see reflection questions. Sometimes they will be for groups and at other times they will be for your personal reflection. In the spirit of the playbook, we would encourage you to make notes as you use the resources, to capture your learning or even suggest how you might improve on the play next time! Try this:

- Thinking about facilitated sessions you've been part of in the last year, what methods have you found most effective?
- What have you noticed about how facilitators start and end sessions?
- Which of the seven aspects of learning conversations listed on page 5 might a method such as diamond nine actively promote?
- Drawing on your own repertoire of facilitation techniques, which methods might you choose to develop any of the list of seven aspects of learning conversations?

Your reflection notes

Do spend some time searching for facilitation techniques and start to build a list of the ones you find helpful.

The playbook is, to mix our metaphors, the tip of an iceberg. Throughout, you'll see QR codes linking to material on the playbook website. Now, it's time to start warming up those creativity and creative thinking muscles!

6 | Creative Thinking in Schools

PART 1

WARMING UP

Warm-Up 1
Explore Creativity and Creative Thinking

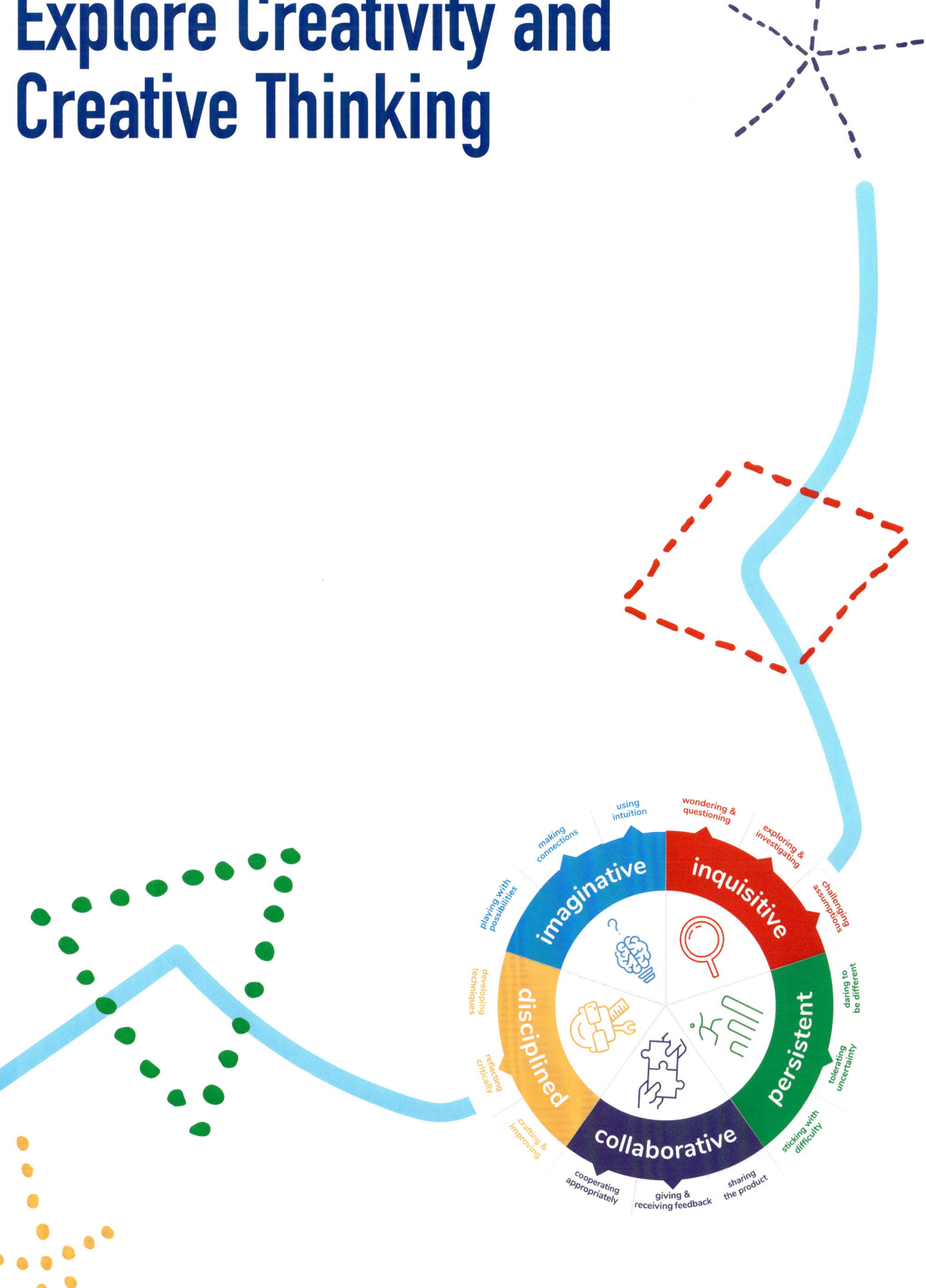

Activity 1
Understand the Essence of Creativity

1 hour

This activity might develop your creative habit of being ...

- inquisitive
- persistent
- collaborative
- disciplined
- imaginative

Developing techniques
Reflecting critically

Purpose

In order to focus on developing the creativity of children and young people in schools, it's essential to have a shared understanding of what it means to be creative. This activity provides a summary of the long history of creativity research in relation to education. You'll learn about the degree to which there's consensus on the meaning of creativity and what it entails. You'll also be presented with a helpful framework for understanding the habits of a creative thinker. This key reading is aimed at creative leaders and others at all levels of the organisation.

Resources and setting up

- Resource 1: Five Creative Habits Framework
- Resource 2: Descriptions of the Creative Habits

Getting going

STEP 1 20 minutes

Read the material and take some time to consider the questions for reflection.

What is creativity?

Over the last 70 years, creativity has become an established field of study starting with the pioneering work of Joy Paul Guilford in the middle of the last century.

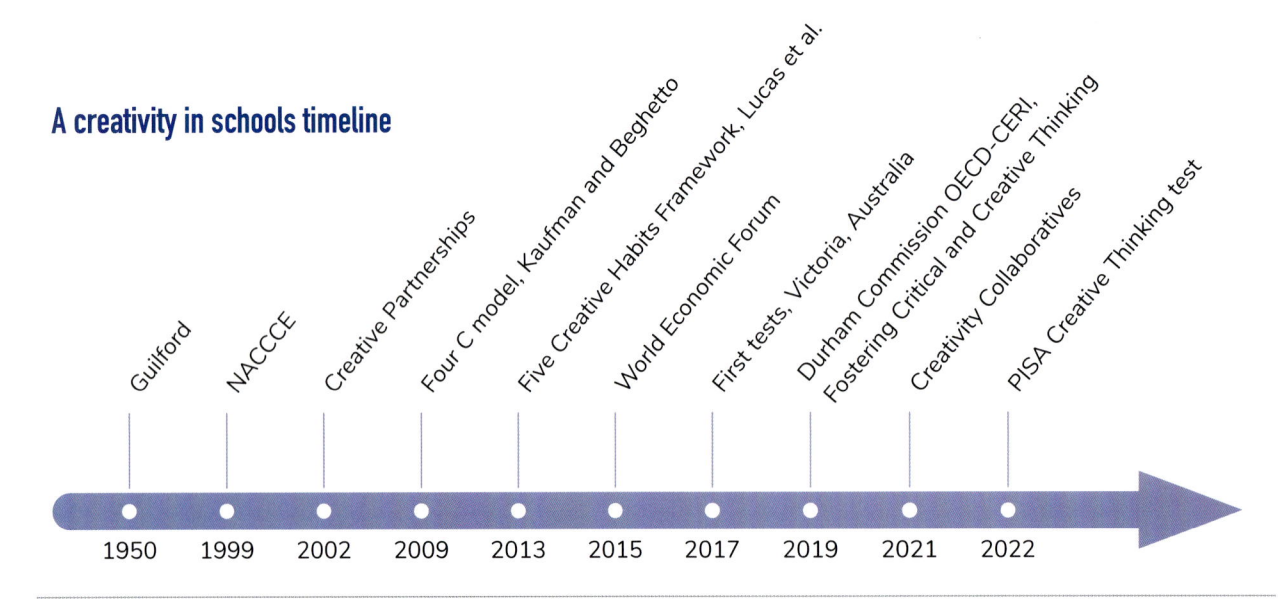

A creativity in schools timeline

1950	Guilford
1999	NACCCE
2002	Creative Partnerships
2009	Four C model, Kaufman and Beghetto
2013	Five Creative Habits Framework, Lucas et al.
2015	World Economic Forum
2017	First tests, Victoria, Australia
2019	Durham Commission OECD-CERI, Fostering Critical and Creative Thinking
2021	Creativity Collaboratives
2022	PISA Creative Thinking test

10 | Warm-Up 1 **Explore Creativity and Creative Thinking**

Guilford suggested that there are two kinds of thinking – *convergent* (coming up with one good idea) and *divergent* (generating multiple solutions).[1] In 1970, Ellis Paul Torrance took the idea of divergent thinking and developed an additional element, elaboration, which meant systematising and organising ideas in greater detail.[2] He developed one of the best known tests of creative thinking using these ingredients.[3] Creativity is both a product (such as an invention) and a process (the methods by which new thinking is achieved).

While there are a growing number of researchers promoting creativity in education, there are few definitions that are universally adopted in schools today. An important milestone occurred at the end of the 20th century with the publication in England of a report by the National Advisory Committee on Creative and Cultural Education (NACCCE).[4] For many teachers, creativity had seemed daunting because of its apparent connection with the leaps of imagination associated with the heights of scientific, mathematical or artistic imagination or innovation. NACCCE defined creativity as 'imaginative activity fashioned so as to produce outcomes that are both original and of value',[5] and this definition was a significant moment in the evolution of English (and international) education.

In 2001, Anna Craft helpfully focused attention on the kind of creativity needed in schools today; what she called 'little c' or everyday creativity – the capacity to generate ideas when necessary.[6] Craft's distinction is echoed by James Kaufman and Ronald Beghetto's Four C model that includes mini-c, little-c, Pro-c and Big-C.[7]

PISA developed a new test of creative thinking administered for the first time in 2022 across 66 countries,[8] alongside its well-known test of reading, maths and science. PISA defines creative thinking as 'the competence to engage productively in the generation, evaluation and improvement of ideas, that can result in original and effective solutions, advances in knowledge and impactful expressions of imagination',[9] which demonstrates that creativity and creative thinking can be used almost interchangeably. In England, again, the Durham Commission on Creativity and Education's definition of teaching for creativity indicates the necessary intentionality of a focus on creativity in schools:

Creativity: The capacity to imagine, conceive, express, or make something that was not there before.

Creative thinking: A process through which knowledge, intuition and skills are applied to imagine, express or make something novel or individual in its contexts. Creative thinking is present in all areas of life. It may appear spontaneous, but it can be underpinned by perseverance, experimentation, critical thinking and collaboration.

Teaching for creativity: Explicitly using pedagogies and practices that cultivate creativity in young people.[10]

---

1 J. P. Guilford, Creativity. *American Psychologist,* 5(9) (1950): 444–454.
2 E. Torrance, *Encouraging Creativity in the Classroom* (Dubuque, IA: William C. Brown, 1970).
3 E. Torrance, *The Torrance Tests of Creative Thinking: Norms-Technical Manual. Research Edition. Verbal Tests, Forms A and B. Figural Tests, Forms A and B* (Princeton, NJ: Personnel Press, 1974).
4 National Advisory Committee on Creative and Cultural Education, *All Our Futures: Creativity, Culture and Education.* Report to the Secretary of State for Education and Employment, the Secretary of State for Culture, Media and Sport (London: Department for Education and Employment, 1999). Available at: https://www.creativitycultureeducation.org/publication/all-our-futures-creativity-culture-and-education.
5 National Advisory Committee on Creative and Cultural Education, *All Our Futures*, p. 30.
6 A. Craft, Little c Creativity. In A. Craft, B. Jeffrey and M. Liebling (eds), *Creativity in Education* (London: Continuum, 2001), pp. 45–61.
7 J. Kaufman and R. Beghetto, Beyond Big and Little: The Four C Model of Creativity. *Review of General Psychology*, 13(1) (2009): 1–12.
8 Organisation for Economic Co-operation and Development, *Thinking Outside the Box: The PISA 2022 Creative Thinking Assessment* (Paris: OECD Publishing, 2022). Available at: https://issuu.com/oecd.publishing/docs/thinking-outside-the-box.
9 Organisation for Economic Co-operation and Development, *PISA 2021: Creative Thinking Framework*, p. 8.
10 Arts Council England and Durham University, *Durham Commission on Creativity and Education*, p. 2.

A framework of creativity and creative habits of mind

Very few frameworks of creativity are specifically designed for schools. The framework developed by the Centre for Real-World Learning at the University of Winchester is one used widely in secondary and primary schools.[11] Selected as the starting point for a four-year, multi-country study by the OECD's Centre for Educational Research and Innovation,[12] it's in use in more than 30 countries across the world. It provided the main case study example in the Durham Commission's report[13] and was significant in building the case for creative thinking being the focus of the 2022 PISA Creative Thinking test.

The framework (see **Resource 1: Five Creative Habits Framework**) has five core creative habits, each of which is composed of three sub-habits. It was explicitly developed for and trialled in English schools as part of the work of Creative Partnerships.[14]

In the framework, creative pupils are:

- **Inquisitive:** good at uncovering and pursuing interesting and worthwhile questions in their creative domain. They wonder, question, explore, investigate and challenge assumptions.

- **Persistent:** not giving up easily. They stick with difficulty, dare to be different and are able to tolerate uncertainty, recognising that certainty isn't always possible or helpful.

- **Collaborative:** seeing the value of teamwork. They acknowledge the social dimension of the creative process, value the sharing of creative products and processes, are able to give and receive feedback, and cooperate appropriately as needed (though not necessarily all the time).

- **Disciplined:** recognising the need for developing knowledge and skill in shaping the creative product and in developing expertise. They know how to improve techniques, reflect critically, and constantly seek to craft and improve what they're creating, taking pride in their work, attending to details and correcting errors.

- **Imaginative:** able to come up with imaginative ideas and solutions. They play with possibilities, make new connections, synthesise ideas and use their intuition as well as their analytical skills.

This framework helps school leaders to understand what habits to focus on as you look to develop the creativity of your pupils (and staff). **Resource 1** and **Resource 2** are two reference guides. **Resource 1** shows the framework and **Resource 2** gives a fuller list of the sub-habits for each of the five habits.

Why do we need creativity in schools?

Over the last two decades, a significant convergence of opinion has emerged as to the value of creativity in education, with employers, psychologists, educationalists and policymakers in most countries across the world recognising the many benefits to young people of cultivating creativity in schools. Such a meeting of minds as to the value of creativity is a relatively recent phenomenon. The case for creativity in schools is multidimensional:

- **Wellbeing.** The connections between personal fulfilment, wellbeing and creativity have been known for a long while. Meanwhile, the reported life satisfaction of UK school pupils was 6.16 – below the OECD average of 7.04,[15] and, according to England's Department for Education, wellbeing declines as children

---

11. B. Lucas, G. Claxton and E. Spencer, *Progression in Student Creativity in School: First Steps Towards New Forms of Formative Assessments.* OECD Education Working Papers No. 86 (Paris: OECD Publishing, 2013). Available at: https://www.oecd.org/education/ceri/5k4dp59msdwk.pdf; B. Lucas, A Five-Dimensional Model of Creativity and its Assessment in Schools. *Applied Measurement in Education*, 29(4) (2016): 278–290.
12. S. Vincent-Lancrin, C. González-Sancho, M. Bouckaert, F. de Luca, M. Fernandez-Barrerra, G. Jacotin, J. Urgel, and Q. Vidal, *Fostering Students' Creativity and Critical Thinking: What It Means in School* (Paris: OECD Publishing, 2019).
13. Arts Council England and Durham University, *Durham Commission on Creativity and Education*, pp. 66–67.
14. See https://www.creativitycultureeducation.org/programme/creative-partnerships.
15. Organisation for Economic Co-operation and Development, *PISA 2018 Results: What School Life Means for Students' Lives* (Volume III) (Paris: OECD Publishing, 2019), p. 322. Available at: https://www.oecd-ilibrary.org/education/pisa-2018-results-volume-iii_acd78851-en.

and young people get older.[16] Mihaly Csikszentmihalyi coined the term 'flow' to describe a state of total absorption in an engaging task.[17] He found flow to be an ingredient of many creative activities and went on to show that flow is highly correlated with subjective wellbeing or happiness. Some progressive governments are also appreciating the power of creativity in supporting wellbeing. Ireland – a 10-year investment in the Creative Ireland programme spanning all government departments – is leading the charge in this regard.[18]

- **Employability.** Among a growing number of global employer organisations, the World Economic Forum has argued for a number of years that, beyond foundational literacies such as literacy, numeracy and science, creativity is one of a number of desirable competences which, along with certain character qualities, describe the range of skills employees will need to thrive today.[19] More recently, as Christopher Petrie noted in *Spotlight: Creativity*, creativity was recorded as 'the #1 top skill by Linkedin.com for the second year in a row'.[20]

- **Economic growth.** Just as creativity and its associated skills are valuable to employees seeking employment, so too are they increasingly associated with economic growth. In the UK, the Confederation of British Industry has argued that the development of creativity is essential for entrepreneurship and innovation. While inherent tensions are found in debates about creativity – such as the degree to which an economic imperative becomes the main (and for some, off-putting) driving force in the policy discourse relating to creativity – the capacity to have a good idea and make new connections has served human beings well in many domains of life and for many centuries.

- **A changing world.** While human beings have always had to deal with uncertainty and weigh up their choices, a review by Rebecca Tauritz observes scholarly consensus about the particular need 'in our rapidly changing world' for young people to develop a series of skills and attitudes to deal with uncertainty.[21] In fast-changing times, we need young people who can generate ideas and think critically if we're to make progress with some of the challenging issues we face globally today. Lynda Gratton and Andrew Scott have shown how creativity and learning, especially the ability to unlearn and rethink, are essential skills, as there's the ever-increasing prospect of many people living to the age of 100.[22]

- **International impetus.** Across the world, many education systems are making progress with fostering creativity, including Australia, a number of states in Canada, Finland and Singapore. From 102 countries reviewed, the kinds of skills associated with creativity are mentioned by 76 countries.[23]

- **Educational benefits more broadly.** In thinking about the case for creativity, it's easy to omit the obvious argument, namely that creativity is a public and personal good in itself. In this last aspect of the case for creativity lies the opportunity for school leaders to take a decision not simply based on conventional evidence but also on values – that a society needs young people with certain habits of mind who also love knowledge and are skilful, and to recognise that such a blend of knowledge, skills and attributes is a powerful goal of schooling.

---

16 Department for Education, *State of the Nation 2019: Children's and Young People's Wellbeing*. Research Report (October 2019), p. 8. Ref: DfE-00203-2019. Available at: https://www.gov.uk/government/publications/state-of-the-nation-2019-children-and-young-peoples-wellbeing.
17 M. Csikszentmihalyi, *Creativity: Flow and the Psychology of Discovery and Invention* (New York: HarperCollins, 1996).
18 See https://www.creativeireland.gov.ie/en.
19 World Economic Forum, *New Vision for Education: Unlocking the Potential of Technology* (2015). Available at: https://www3.weforum.org/docs/WEFUSA_NewVisionforEducation_Report2015.pdf.
20 C. Petrie, *Spotlight: Creativity* (Helsinki: HundrED, 2020), p. 10.
21 R. Tauritz, A Pedagogy for Uncertain Times. In W. Lambrechts and J. Hindson (eds), *Research and Innovation in Education for Sustainable Development: Exploring Collaborative Networks, Critical Characteristics and Evaluation Practices* (Vienna: Environment and School Initiatives, 2016), pp. 90–105 at p. 90.
22 L. Gratton and A. Scott, *The 100-Year Life: Living and Working in an Age of Longevity* (London: Bloomsbury, 2016).
23 E. Care, K. Anderson and H. Kim, *Visualizing the Breadth of Skills Movement Across Education Systems* (Washington, DC: Brookings Institution, 2016). Available at: https://www.brookings.edu/research/visualizing-the-breadth-of-skills-movement-across-education-systems.

STEP 2 15 minutes

Share your initial thoughts with another person or small group before getting together with the whole group.

Reflecting together

STEP 3 25 minutes

- Which words used in the definitions seem to you most strongly associated with creativity?
- Which of the benefits seem most important to you in the context of your school?
- What would you say to a sceptical colleague who suggests that creativity is too vague to teach?
- What would you say to a pupil to explain why you believe developing their creativity will help them in school and in life?

Your reflection notes

Warm-Up 1 **Explore Creativity and Creative Thinking**

Activity 2
Find the Creative You

🕐 1 hour

This activity might develop your creative habit of being ...

Exploring & investigating (inquisitive)

Cooperating appropriately / Giving & receiving feedback / Sharing the product (collaborative)

Reflecting critically (disciplined)

Purpose

Myths surrounding creativity and educators' perceptions about their own capacity to be creative can be a common barrier when considering broader pedagogical approaches. This activity aims to highlight your existing strengths, skills, knowledge, experiences and qualities and explore how they might complement the five creative habits.

Resources and setting up

- Large sheets of paper or flip chart paper taped together – large enough for each participant to have an outline of their body drawn
- Different-coloured pens and marker pens
- **Resource 1: Five Creative Habits Framework**
- **Resource 2: Descriptions of the Creative Habits**
- Encourage participants to work with someone they don't know well or don't work with regularly
- This activity assumes you've read **Activity 1: Understand the Essence of Creativity**

Getting going

STEP 1 5 minutes

Working in pairs, draw around each other's bodies on the paper.

STEP 2 15 minutes

Working individually, fill your outlined body with the strengths, skills, knowledge, experiences and qualities you possess and bring to your work. Think about where on your body the strengths are located and plot them in place – for example, passion for your work might be in your heart or your questioning skills might be near your mouth.

STEP 3 10 minutes

Share the outline drawing of your body with your partner, explaining what you've drawn or written and why. You'll need to listen carefully to each other to be able to complete the next step.

STEP 4 15 minutes

Come back together as a whole group. In turn, everyone introduces their partner's drawing and talks about their strengths, skills, knowledge, experiences and qualities. As you listen to each person talk, you should all think about where the creative habits can be identified – referring to **Resources 1** and **2**.

Reflecting together

STEP 5 15 minutes

- Where and how have the creative habits featured in your strengths, skills, knowledge, experiences and qualities?
- Which one of the five creative habits is more like you? Which one is least like you?
- Has this activity challenged any previous assumptions about your own creativity?
- Has this activity helped to affirm your creative identity as a leader/educator? If so, how?
- What does this mean for you as an educator and for you as a team?

Your reflection notes

16 | Warm-Up 1 **Explore Creativity and Creative Thinking**

Activity 3
Explore Creative Habits

1 hour

This activity might develop your creative habit of being ...

- **inquisitive** — Wondering & questioning, Exploring & investigating, Challenging assumptions
- **persistent** — Tolerating uncertainty 
- **collaborative** — Cooperating appropriately, Giving & receiving feedback 
- **disciplined** — Reflecting critically 
- **imaginative** — Making connections, Using intuition 

Purpose

It's essential to develop a shared understanding of what creativity is. This activity helps you to explore the creative habits and their sub-habits using the Five Creative Habits Framework. It can also be easily adapted to fit with your own definition. It helps people to investigate and develop a shared understanding of what creativity is and to examine their own creative habits, including their strengths and potential development needs.

Resources and setting up

- **Resource 1: Five Creative Habits Framework**
- **Resource 3: Creativity Habits Web Template** (one for each person)
- **Resource 4: Creative Individuals Are ...** (one of these sheets for each group of four or five). Each sheet includes one creative habit and its three sub-habits
- Felt pen or marker pen (one for each person)
- Rolls of different-coloured electrical tape (one roll for each person)
- Masking tape (one roll for each small group of four or five)
- Scissors (two pairs for each small group)

Refer to the image and set up the creativity webs on the floor in advance of the activity. Use:

- The masking tape to create the creativity webs on the floor.
- A marker pen (to write 1, 2, 3, 4 and 5 on each axis with 1 being closest to the centre and 5 at the outside).
- The five sheets from **Resource 4** that detail the sub-habits for each creative habit. One of the five creative habits is placed at the end of each axis of the web, using **Resource 3** to ensure they're placed in the correct order.

Place a set of coloured tape and two pairs of scissors near each creativity web.

Activity 3 **Explore Creative Habits** | 17

Getting going

STEP 1 10 minutes

Everyone has a creativity habits web template (Resource 3) and a felt pen/marker pen.

Working individually, plot your own creativity on the template. Reflecting on each of the creative habits and their sub-habits, rate how creative you are using a scale of 1–5 (1 = only beginning, 5 = advanced).

Think about specific examples and evidence of when/where you've been using each of the creative habits and their sub-habits. Write your examples next to the relevant creative habit on the creativity web.

It's important to rate yourselves honestly; think about your strengths and identify where you feel there's room to develop and grow your creativity. Do this individually, and try not to talk about or share your creativty habits web template with others.

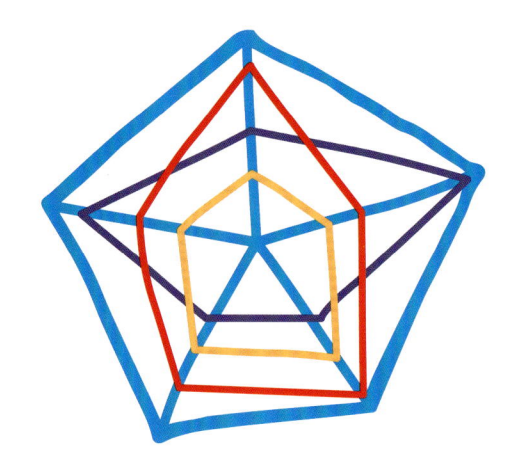

STEP 2 20–25 minutes

In small groups of four or five, move to one of the creativity webs on the floor.

Make sure each of your group members has a different colour of tape. Use this to recreate your own creativity web on the floor.

In your groups, everyone presents their creativity web, explaining the reasons for each rating and sharing relevant examples as evidence of the ratings.

Take a photograph of your finished creativity webs for sharing and reflecting with the wider school.

Reflecting together

STEP 3 20–25 minutes

- How has this activity challenged your understanding of creativity?
- What development needs and priorities has this activity revealed?
- Why is understanding your own creativity important for developing pupils' creativity?
- How might you model these creative habits as leaders, teachers and colleagues?
- Where in your practice and classroom dialogue are these creative habits currently present?
- In planning learning, how might you create opportunities to develop these skills and reflect on pupils' progress?
- Why are these creative habits important to develop in your children and young people?
- Did looking at how others rated themselves change your personal opinion at all?

Your reflection notes

18 | Warm-Up 1 **Explore Creativity and Creative Thinking**

Activity 4
Chart Your Creativity Over Time

30 minutes

This activity might develop your creative habit of being ...

inquisitive · persistent · collaborative · **Reflecting critically** · **Using intuition**

Purpose

Modelling creativity is about showing that you embrace new thinking and risk-taking and are willing to learn from your mistakes as a leader. This activity invites you to self-assess your disposition towards creative thinking in your role, and to do so at various stages as your experience and confidence progresses. Individual-level change is essential for leadership. This activity is ongoing and something that happens as long as you're leading for creativity.

Resources and setting up

- Resource 2: Descriptions of the Creative Habits

Getting going

This is an individual journaling and 'microblogging' task. A microblog is a short blog post, typically 140–280 characters, that can be written or received on a range of devices, including a smartphone. The quick journaling activity supports your habits of imagination and allows you to take a step back in order to assess your development from a more detached stance.

STEP 1 10 minutes

Look at the table on page 20 and select one of the five creative habits and its sub-habits. You might wish to refer to Resource 2, although the purpose of this activity isn't to overthink but to use your intuition. Immediately begin to write in response to the questions that appear in the corresponding right-hand column.

Activity 4 **Chart Your Creativity Over Time** | 19

Inquisitive	Where and how is wondering and questioning in your leadership practice currently?
	In what ways do you make time to explore and investigate issues more deeply?
	Who might agree with you that you challenge your assumptions?
Persistent	When have you had to tolerate uncertainty recently, and how did this make you feel?
	What example do you have of sticking with difficulty in the past week?
	How have you dared to be different, and what was the reaction?
Collaborative	When have you given feedback on the ideas of others/received feedback on your ideas in the past week, and what was the outcome?
	What recent examples do you have of cooperating appropriately, and what was the impact?
	What products have you shared, and how were they received by others?
Disciplined	In what ways have you reflected critically in the past 24 hours?
	How are you developing a range of techniques for thinking creatively?
	What examples do you have of crafting and improving during the last two weeks, and what were the challenges?
Imaginative	How have you played with possibilities recently, and what was the outcome?
	What connections have you made between ideas, and what were the difficulties in doing so?
	When have you made a conscious decision to use your intuition, and how did it feel?

Write continuously in response to the questions for five minutes. Once you've written for five minutes, read over what you've written and identify the words that jump out at you. What do these words tell you about your strengths? Your areas for development? Then consider what this has surfaced for you – what has surprised you?

This isn't a standalone task. We encourage you to do this task at the beginning of your journey and repeat it regularly, tracking your progress and challenging your thinking over time.

After you've written in your journal three to four times, reflect on your writing and identify where you see changes in your practice and how it's visible to others.

STEP 2 20 minutes

Use some text from your journal entries in combination with your reflections and share them as a microblog to demonstrate how you're valuing and investing in your creativity and to inspire others to follow your example.

You might like to allocate a specific amount of time to set aside for reflection at key points as you progress in your focus on creativity and creative thinking.

Your reflection notes

Activity 5
Notice Creativity in Action

1 hour 15 minutes

This activity might develop your creative habit of being . . .

inquisitive	persistent	collaborative	disciplined	imaginative
Wondering & questioning Exploring & investigating Challenging assumptions	Tolerating uncertainty	Giving & receiving feedback	Reflecting critically	Making connections

Purpose

Often, elements of creative thinking already exist in school curricula, pedagogy and assessment but they're undetected. Making a conscious effort to notice creative thinking is a significant step towards valuing it and understanding how to move forward. This activity explores where creativity is being cultivated in your school(s) and considers how leaders can continue to support it and build on current strengths.

Resources and setting up

You'll need an even number of groups with space for groups to work on tables or on the floor. Each group will need a set of the following resources:

- A copy of each of the five posters contained in **Resource 4: Creative Individuals Are ...** You'll assign individuals to a group looking at one of the five sub-habits. Groups of three to five would work well, so multiply the number of copies accordingly.
- **Resource 5: Curriculum, Pedagogy and Assessment/Progression Venn**.
- Marker pens in red, blue and green (one each for assessment, pedagogy and curriculum).
- Five sheets of flip chart paper.
- Glue or sticky tape.
- Glue or tape each of the **Resource 4** posters to a sheet of flip chart paper at the top as a reference.

On each piece of flip chart paper, write the three sub-habits for one of the five creative habits. Space them out, allowing room for comments around each word.

Getting going

Working in groups, imagine you're preparing for a visit by a fictitious 'creativity investigation team'. The investigators want to see where the development of creative thinking is currently present/visible in your curriculum, assessment and pedagogy. Each group will focus on a single creative habit.

STEP 1 35 minutes

In groups clustered around one of each of the five habits (as shown on the **Resource 4** posters) refer to **Resource 5**. Using the corresponding colour marker pen for curriculum, assessment and pedagogy, record what you would show the creativity investigation team against each of your allocated creative habit's sub-habits.

Consider the following:

- Where in the school would you take them and why?
- What would you show them and why?
- Which areas of the curriculum would you show them?
- What would they see?
- What materials would you share with them and why?

For example, if your group receives the **Resource 4** poster related to 'inquisitive', start to populate the flip chart paper with evidence written in red (assessment), blue (pedagogy) and green (curriculum) of each of the sub-habits being developed.

Key Stage 3 science might come to mind first. Next to 'Wondering and questioning' you might write in red, 'KS3 Science: Exhibition of projects as the focus of assessment. Use of gallery critique where peers post questions on one another's work to help improve it.' Next to 'Exploring and investigating' you might write in blue, 'KS3 Science: Use of problem-based learning to explore why certain areas in the school grounds are more likely to attract wildlife.'

Where there are gaps, you might think about other areas of the curriculum that could provide evidence.

Going deeper

STEP 2 15 minutes

Now think about how you could encourage this kind of detailed noticing of the fifteen sub-habits in classrooms across the school relating to curriculum, pedagogy and assessment. You might like to use a wall in the staffroom with some worked examples for other colleagues to consider.

STEP 3 10 minutes

In pairs, share your work with another group.

Reflecting together

STEP 4 15 minutes

- Was there consensus about what you would show the investigation team? If so, why and where?
- What does this tell you about the areas you didn't choose to show the team?
- Where are your strengths (which colour appears the most)? Why do you think that's the case, and what role have leaders had in supporting this?
- What needs to change, and what can leaders do to support this change?
- What are your priority next steps?

Your reflection notes

Warm-Up 1 **Explore Creativity and Creative Thinking**

Warm-Up 2
Shift the Paradigm

Activity 6
Be Clear About the Purpose of School

🕐 1 hour 20 minutes

This activity might develop your creative habit of being ...

Wondering & questioning
Exploring & investigating
Challenging assumptions

Sticking with difficulty

Cooperating appropriately
Sharing the product

Crafting & improving
Reflecting critically

Making connections

Purpose

Lack of clarity about the purpose of education can lead you to focus on things of little value. This activity, which could be for the whole-school community, serves as a useful launch pad to begin a dialogue about creative thinking in education, what this might mean, how it might be evolving and how creativity underpins a more expansive philosophy about the purpose of school. It also surfaces people's values and provides an opportune moment to unravel tensions within your setting if there are broad differences in responses.

Resources and setting up

- A set of 15 A5 cards for each table
- Felt pens/marker pens for each table
- Arrange tables and chairs for small groups of around four

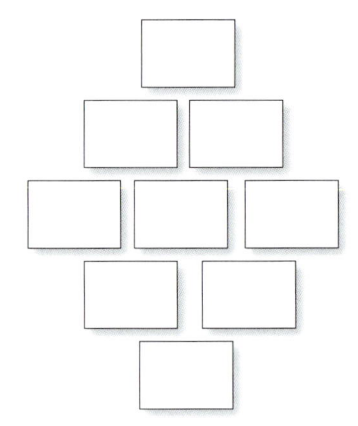

Getting going

STEP 1 20 minutes

Working in groups around tables, the participants begin by considering the question, 'What is the purpose of school?' After an initial conversation, collectively come up with 15 statements summarising the most important purposes of school. Write each of these on one of the cards. After 20 minutes, each rotate to another table, leaving your cards behind.

STEP 2 10 minutes

At your new table, each consider the 15 statements and remove the six you consider the least important. Again, the cards are left as each group rotates to another table.

Warm-Up 2 **Shift the Paradigm**

STEP 3 10 minutes

Arrange the final nine statements into a diamond formation with the *most important* at the top and the *least important* at the bottom, as shown below.

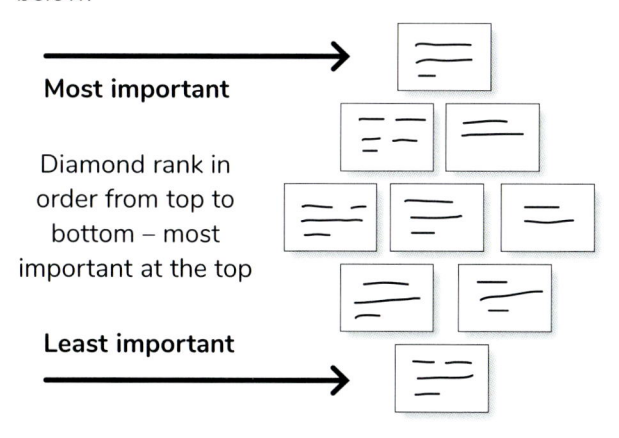

Most important

Diamond rank in order from top to bottom – most important at the top

Least important

STEP 4 10 minutes

Return to your original tables to talk about what you find and to consider the following questions:

- Have you lost anything significant in the six statements that were rejected?
- Would you bring any of them back into the diamond nine? Why?
- Are you happy with the ranking of the nine remaining statements? What would you change and why?

STEP 5 10 minutes

Nominate someone to share the views of the group on the questions above. In sharing these views, explain your group's conclusions.

Reflecting together

STEP 6 20 minutes

- Is there a broad consensus as to what is the purpose of school? What are the similarities and differences? What do you do about the differences?
- How has the purpose of your school changed in the last 10 years?
- What do the outcomes of this activity mean for your school and your vision?
- What do you need to stop, start and/or amplify to support your school to realise this purpose?
- What are your next steps?

Your reflection notes

Activity 7
A Different Kind of School

1 hour 15 minutes

This activity might develop your creative habit of being …

Daring to be different **Giving & receiving feedback** **Making connections Playing with possibilities**

Purpose

Schools that are learning organisations are better equipped to face the twists and turns that accompany complex changes. This activity helps you to consider what it means to be a learning organisation and explore the kind of school that's most likely to support and nurture creative thinking.

Resources and setting up

- One copy of **Resource 6: Schools as Learning Organisations: Stimulating Environments for Creative Thinking** for each participant

- For each small group, access to a copy of the OECD's *What Makes a School a Learning Organisation? A Guide for Policy Makers, School Leaders and Teachers*[1]

- Large sheets and pens

- **Resource 7: School as a Learning Organisation Plan**

Getting going

STEP 1 10 minutes

Read **Resource 6**.

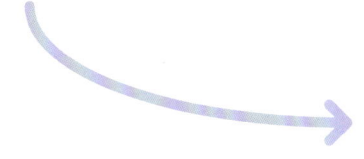

STEP 2 10 minutes

Get into groups of three or four. First, reflect together on this question:

- What is it about a school as a learning organisation (SLO) that's likely to help people develop curricula, pedagogies and assessments to promote and embed creative thinking habits?

---

1 Organisation for Economic Co-operation and Development, *What Makes a School a Learning Organisation? A Guide for Policy Makers, School Leaders and Teachers* (Paris: OECD Publishing, 2016). Available at: https://www.oecd.org/education/school/school-learning-organisation.pdf.

26 | Warm-Up 2 **Shift the Paradigm**

Going deeper

STEP 3 15 minutes

Next, thinking about developing creative thinking in your school(s), in your group select one SLO dimension to focus on, making sure that all the dimensions are covered. **Resource 7** contains an image of all seven dimensions of the SLO, followed by a template that allows you to make notes on a single dimension of your choice. Using your reading about the dimension (you can find more information about the elements in the OECD publication), make a list on the template or on a large sheet of paper. Include in your list:

- Things you could do to develop that dimension.
- Resources and support needed, if any (including time).
- Challenges you anticipate and thoughts about addressing these.

STEP 4 15 minutes

Each group now selects one of the creative habits or sub-habits which you'll use as a particular lens for your learning conversation.

Get together with a group working on a different dimension. Compare your SLO plans, acting as critical friends to help each other extend your thinking. Take it in turns to explore the dimension you've each been working on.

STEP 5 10 minutes

As a whole group, briefly share one activity each.

Your reflection notes

Reflecting together

STEP 6 15 minutes

- What have you learned about your school as a learning organisation from this activity?
- What strengths and development opportunities have you noticed in your school?
- As you think about your school, what is the end you have in mind (i.e. in terms of creative thinking)? What is your big-picture vision for the school?
- What are your next steps?

Activity 7 **A Different Kind of School** | 27

Activity 8
A Different Kind of Leadership

50 minutes

This activity might develop your creative habit of being …

Giving & receiving feedback

Developing techniques Crafting & improving

Purpose

While school leadership has been extensively researched in general terms, leadership that's explicitly designed to cultivate creative thinking in education has not. This reading is about the mind shift that's needed to make it clear that creative leadership isn't 'business as usual'. By then asking you to interpret your own school's efforts in the light of your reading, we're inviting you to demonstrate your own creative leadership in action.

Getting going

STEP 1 10 minutes

All read the following:

The nature of school leadership

There's a rich literature base on effective school leadership.[1] The ultimate aim of school leadership is to make a powerful difference to the lives of children and young people by engaging others in preparing them for their future. In some schools and systems, this can be interpreted as what school leaders do to boost educational outcomes for pupils. Our own literature review suggests that, when focusing on the development of creativity and creative thinking across a whole school, the challenges are greater than this narrow definition implies.[2] Louise Stoll argues that leaders will also need to have an interest 'in exploring and developing conditions in which colleagues feel able to take risks, inquire into stubborn problems, explore potential learning strategies, experiment, innovate, fail and use failure for learning'.[3]

This takes us into reimagining leadership for creativity. In this short reading, we consider some of the reasons why creative leadership is more than 'good' leadership in schools. We define creative leadership as that which:

> … explicitly develops the creativity of all of its members, staff and pupils alike. Creative leaders ensure that there are multiple opportunities for developing the creativity of all young people while at the same time recognising that for a school truly to be a creative organisation then developing the creativity of its leaders *and* staff is important both as a means to an end and as an end in itself.[4]

---

1 K. Leithwood, A. Harris and D. Hopkins, Seven Strong Claims About Successful School Leadership Revisited. *School Leadership & Management*, 40(1) (2020): 5–22.
2 B. Lucas, E. Spencer and L. Stoll, *Creative Leadership to Develop Creativity and Creative Thinking in English Schools: A Review of the Evidence* (London: The Mercers' Company, 2021). Available at: https://www.creativityexchange.org.uk/asset/223.
3 L. Stoll, Creative Capacity for Learning: Are We There Yet? *Journal of Educational Change*, 21(3) (2020): 421–430 at 427.
4 Lucas et al., *Creative Leadership to Develop Creativity and Creative Thinking in English Schools*, p. 28.

Creative school leadership

Why might leading a school in which the creativity of pupils and staff is a priority be any different from leading a school to improve pupil outcomes, or in which the achievement of vision and goals is the focus of attention? One obvious challenge is the need to integrate curriculum, pedagogy and assessment and have a sense of what pupils' progression in creative thinking looks like, as in the model below:

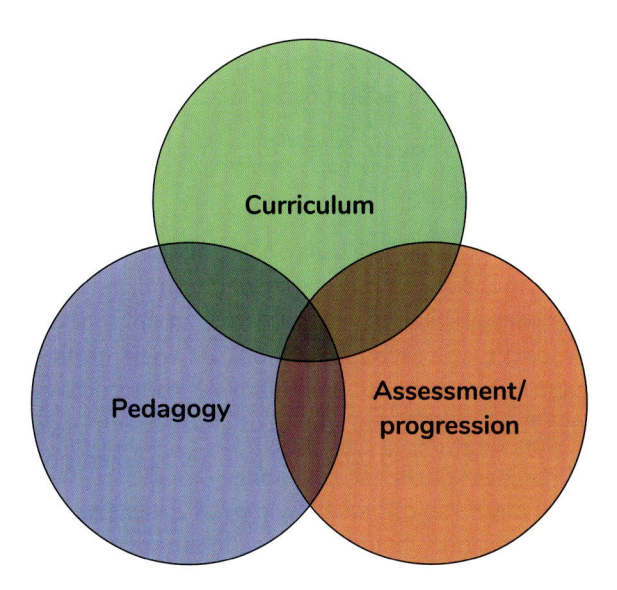

[Venn diagram showing three overlapping circles: Curriculum, Pedagogy, and Assessment/progression]

Each of the three elements has its challenges. There's no accepted curriculum for creative thinking; it needs to be embedded in every subject. While there's a growing awareness of the kinds of pedagogies that are most effective, many school leaders may not be familiar with these. The assessment of creative thinking is very much in its infancy,[5] and levels of confidence and capability among teachers are unsurprisingly low. And there's as yet no widely accepted description of pupil progression in creative thinking, although some countries such as Australia have attempted this.[6]

Leadership for teachers' creative development

Let's look at what happens in the classroom – the focus of much leadership endeavour in schools. For teachers, the challenge here is how to teach a subject and a habit of mind. 'Split screen teaching' is the simple but powerful idea that you need to weave opportunities for creative thinking into every subject of the school curriculum and do so intentionally: science + collaboration, maths + inquisitiveness, history + imagination and so on. It invites teachers to describe two worlds: the disciplinary subject matter of their lesson *and* the creative habit on which they're also focusing.

To do this requires a different approach to curriculum planning, explicitly interleaving aspects of creativity with elements of a specific subject. This in turn calls for greater attention on the selection of teaching methods or signature pedagogies (as we explore in **Activity 23**). Such pedagogies include problem-based and inquiry-led learning, role play and simulation, jigsaw methods, thinking routines and deliberate practice.

A signature pedagogy is a distinctive way of teaching selected with a particular outcome in mind. The concept was developed originally in the context of preparing learners for different vocational routes – for example, accounting, midwifery or engineering – by considering the kinds of teaching that would work best to train them for their new professions. In our case, we're inviting teachers to consider which pedagogies will develop creative thinkers. How can we cultivate scientists who know how to cooperate appropriately,

---

5 B. Lucas, *A Field Guide to Assessing Creative Thinking in Schools* (Perth: FORM, 2022). Available at: https://drive.google.com/file/d/19WiqUOHWgODLSxDID4RnMMD0-25dJa5F/view.
6 See https://www.australiancurriculum.edu.au/f-10-curriculum/general-capabilities/critical-and-creative-thinking.

mathematicians who wonder and question, and historians who use their intuition? In the case of creative thinking, this will be a combination of one of the five habits and an aspect of the relevant programme of study.

Teachers find this hard. And leaders have to step to one side from more performance-driven, evidence-informed approaches – for example, effective teaching of phonics or grammar in English or accuracy in maths – to the more existential question of how best to develop creative writers and mathematicians. For school leaders wishing to grow teachers who 'get' this, this is no easy matter.

In addition, there are leadership challenges for promoting new kinds of curriculum design, building teacher assessment confidence and developing a whole suite of school documents to capture the ways in which creativity is being embedded across the school.

Other creative leadership challenges

Beyond the classroom, a host of other challenges exist, of which the following are some examples:

- Creative thinking values originality; the assessment system tends to value 'one right answer'.
- Creative thinking invites us to take risks; schools have to manage and, in some senses, discourage risk-taking.
- Exercising our creative thinking can mean adopting radical new positions; these can put us at loggerheads with existing practices and out on a limb.
- Creativity is invisible in most school assessment and reporting systems.
- Creativity is frequently largely invisible to external inspection systems such as Ofsted in England or Estyn in Wales, and to departments or ministries of education.
- Creativity comes freighted with baggage – the myths that those who are threatened by it seek to highlight (see **Activity 18: Debunk Myths About Creativity**).

Going deeper

STEP 2 30 minutes

Your school is being visited by a group of senior leaders from other schools who have heard that what you're doing in embedding creativity in your school is interesting.

What would you say to the visiting leaders that explains how 'creative leadership' is different from 'good leadership'? What are its signature practices?

Take it in turns to offer your views, and then offer each other feedback.

Reflecting together

STEP 3 10 minutes

- To what extent is your school already demonstrating the signature creative leadership practices described in the reading?
- How do you respond to the other challenges listed above?

Your reflection notes

Activity 9
Creative Leadership in Action

40 minutes

This activity might develop your creative habit of being ...

inquisitive | persistent | collaborative | disciplined | imaginative

Developing techniques
Reflecting critically

Making connections

Purpose

The interrelationship between leader, teacher and pupil creativity gives rise to a set of 'creative leadership plays' in which creative leaders might wish to engage. This activity aims to help you develop a shared understanding of creative leadership in action. It provides a summary of what creative leadership looks like and summarises the key plays it involves. Organised to reflect the structure of the playbook, it guides you through the reading and activities that follow.

Resources and setting up

- **Resource 8: Creative Leadership Plays**
- **Resource 9: Creative Leadership Plays – Notes**

Getting going

STEP 1 25 minutes

This guide to the creative leadership plays can be used as a reference as you engage with the plays. To get the most out of your session, it would be helpful to start by reading the introduction and each of the 10 creative leadership activity summaries that follow before you address the reflection questions.

Introduction

Internationally, interest is growing in the importance of creativity as a learning disposition from which young people can benefit. While there's considerable evidence about effective educational leadership, the way to lead for creativity is less well understood.

Creative leadership is a relatively new and emerging field, and there's no best practice guide to bringing about this change in children and young people's thinking and behaviour. Creative leadership aims to develop the creative thinking and creativity of all pupils. This sort of leadership is relevant to the work of all those involved and interested in leadership in schools, not just principals and other senior leaders.

Both teacher and leadership team creativity are important in developing learner creativity. This means that part of the job of a creative leader is, first, to develop staff creativity, so they can recognise its importance and create opportunities for pupils to develop in the same way. This brings the creative leader's own creativity into focus as well.

Inevitably, the actions of creative leadership in part reflect what we know about 'good' leadership practices, and also what we know about schools that are learning organisations (see **Activity 7: A Different Kind of School**). But the 10 categories of creative leadership play developed throughout this playbook seek to have a distinct impact on creativity; ultimately, the development of creative thinking in all pupils.

Going deeper

The table below lists the 10 categories of creative leadership play and how the related activities aim to help develop creative leadership. Each play is also explained in **Resource 8**.

Play number	Creative leadership plays
1	**The Change Process: Articulate a clear description of the process of change, so everyone understands how young people's creativity will be developed.** The activities in this play introduce you to the idea of a 'theory of change'. When you've worked through the playbook you might wish to revisit this, having taken part in the activities and with a clearer understanding of what each play entails and how it might look in your own organisation. You'll also consider how networks support the change process and the associated challenges and risks.
2	**Develop Leaders: Identify and nurture creative change catalysts/teacher leaders.** This play aims to help you recognise where there are potential 'creative change catalysts' within your organisation. These may not be officially designated leaders, but they're individuals who are enthusiastic about developing creativity and may be developed in their teacher leadership role or become teacher leaders.
3	**Change the Culture: Create a culture in which creativity is promoted and valued in every aspect of the school's life and reflected in the school's improvement plan.** Activities in this play familiarise you with the concept of 'culture' as it relates to the development of creativity in schools. Your school improvement plan is a key document in examining culture. Your school's timetabling, use of space and displays also contain key messages. The play also aims to highlight the importance of modelling creativity. An important aspect of your school's culture is the language used in relation to creativity, and this needs to be consistent. The idea of developing a common language has implications for other creative leadership plays in which you'll engage – for example: • In **Play 3: Change the Culture**, you'll want to ensure the language is agreed and used. • In **Play 6: Rethink Pedagogy**, you'll want to consider which aspects of creativity are best developed within which subjects, and consider selecting the right set of words with which to talk about creativity. • In **Play 7: Track Progression**, you'll want to consider how language is incorporated within assessment structures. You'll examine the five creative habits and their associated language in **Activity 1: Understand the Essence of Creativity**. • In **Play 8: Ensure Professional Learning**, you'll want to explain the language and explore frameworks for understanding creativity contextualised within teachers' own subject area.
4	**Rethink Structures: Build creative thinking into all resourcing.** This play is about school structures, which include the resources of time, money and planning. Plans include those for school improvement, appraisal and timetabling. Activities in this play aim to highlight the benefits of ensuring creative thinking flows through the school improvement plan and the benefits of collaborative planning in the long, medium and short term; to reflect on other elements of planning (e.g. appraisal plan); and to consider other resources.

Play number	Creative leadership plays
5	**Develop a Creative Curriculum: Embed creativity into a coherent curriculum.** The activities in this play help you to establish creativity in planning across all subject areas. The things a school prioritises outside of the academic curriculum are also important here. There are a number of places to introduce creativity and allow for its development other than within subjects. Leadership for creativity involves considering how to incorporate creativity within extra-curricular areas (such as assemblies, discrete lessons and creative days/weeks) and co-curricular activities.
6	**Rethink Pedagogy: Develop staff confidence in using teaching and learning methods that cultivate creativity.** This play helps you to think about developing staff confidence in using teaching and learning methods that cultivate creativity. It draws on the idea of signature pedagogies to show that there are some helpful ways of teaching for creativity within different subject areas.
7	**Track Progression in Creative Thinking: Find ways to assess that explicitly recognise progress in the development of young people's creativity.** Assessing what is valued is important to ensure that it remains in focus. This play aims to help you become familiar with the different methods of assessment currently available.
8	**Ensure Professional Learning: Make creativity a focus of staff professional learning.** An area of activity for creative leaders is in considering how your school's professional development offerings can be used strategically to develop creativity. This play aims to help you develop teachers' ability to consider how creativity fits within their subject.
9	**Collaborate with External Partners: Invest in external partners and funding to help develop creativity.** The activities in this play aim to generate awareness of the importance of links with external organisations, including other schools.
10	**Reflect and Evaluate: Explore, reflect on and evaluate your school's journey to creativity.** Assessment includes evaluation – exploring and reflecting on your school's journey to creativity. This play helps creative leaders to initiate a school-wide, teaching-staff reflection on the school's creativity journey.

You might also choose to talk about a small number of the activities below, in pairs, and feed back to a larger group jigsaw-style (see **An example activity** for an example of the jigsaw approach).

Reflecting together

STEP 2 15 minutes

Having read about the 10 creative leadership plays, you might like to make notes in the table in **Resource 9** as you think about your own school. As you work your way through the playbook, you might wish to reflect back on your thinking as you expand your understanding of each of the creative leadership plays.

- Prior to picking up this playbook, what would you have understood by the term 'creative leadership'?
- How has this activity changed and challenged your understanding of creative leadership?
- What do you think each creativity leadership activity might involve?
- How will this develop teachers' and pupils' creativity?
- To what extent are you doing this already?
- As you think about your school's priorities, what might your next steps be as you work through this playbook?

Your reflection notes

Warm-Up 2 **Shift the Paradigm**

PART 2

PLAYING THE WHOLE GAME OF LEARNING

Play 1
The Change Process

Activity 10
Use a Theory of Change

🕐 1 hour 15 minutes

This activity might develop your creative habit of being …

Tolerating uncertainty

Making connections
Playing with possibilities

Purpose

This activity introduces the idea of a theory of change, explaining how it helps you to understand the steps you need to take to achieve the changes you want to see. It invites you to think about reverse engineering – choosing interventions that will make the most progress towards your desired goal. It also helps you as leaders to think through the assumptions you have about change and the resources you'll need to bring it about.

Resources and setting up

- **Resource 10: Using a Theory of Change in Schools** (copy the planning triangle onto A3 sheets for participants)
- **Resource 11: Intervention Cards**

Getting going

Read **Resource 10** before you start.

STEP 1 15 minutes

Work in groups of three. Each group has a blank planning triangle, a set of cards and the reading (unless this has been pre-work).

Take a simple example to exemplify an intervention, an intermediate outcome and a final goal. Imagine that losing weight is the final goal. An intervention could be eating one fewer meal a day or taking more exercise. These might lead to an intermediate outcome of self-awareness about which weight-loss intervention works for a busy person.

The groups spend three minutes discussing this example and considering other possible interventions and other potential intermediate outcomes.

As a whole group, check that you all understand the core idea of interventions leading to intermediate outcomes leading in turn to a desired goal.

Think about the idea of, 'If we do X then Y will happen, so that we'll achieve Z.' Close this step by putting the weight-loss theory of change into a sentence along the lines of, 'If I start to take exercise and eat one fewer meal a day, then I'll begin to learn how to manage my diet and exercise better and start to lose weight.'

STEP 2 20 minutes

In groups, write 'Creative thinking embedded in every subject/class across the school' (or something similar) in the top part of their triangle.

Lay out the intervention cards and discuss those you think will be most relevant for you and your context. Remove any that you don't wish to consider and create new ones you feel are missing. Choose up to five interventions that you think will contribute towards your desired goal. You'll need to 'defend' your choices to other colleagues in the next step of the activity.

STEP 3 20 minutes

Each group joins another one and shares their choice of interventions. Acting as a critical friend, the other group then suggests what the intermediate outcomes might be as a result of such interventions. Prompts might include ideas such as, 'Increased staff confidence in teaching' or 'Increased understanding by pupils of the language of creativity'. Remember to divide the time equally between your groups.

Each group of three uses the suggestions from the other group to refine their own theory of change planning triangle.

STEP 4 10 minutes

Get into a circle. With your planning triangles in front of you, take it in turns to put your theory of change into a sentence along the lines of:

> 'If we introduce the Five Creative Habits Framework, offer professional learning opportunities on signature pedagogies and create protected time for staff to plan, then staff will feel better prepared to teach for creativity, so it's more likely that creative thinking will be embedded in all subjects of our school's curriculum.'

Reflecting together

STEP 5 10 minutes

- How might using a theory of change help you to be clearer about what you're planning?
- What assumptions are you making about the interventions you've selected?
- What leadership actions are essential to enable the changes you're planning?
- What resources will you need to put your theory of change into action?
- Which interventions will you start with?

You might also like to explore:

Harries, E., Hodgson, L. and Noble, J. (2014) *Creating Your Theory of Change: NPC's Practical Guide*. London: New Philanthropy Capital. Available at: https://www.thinknpc.org/wp-content/uploads/2018/07/Creating-your-theory-of-change1.pdf.

Lucas, B. (2021) *Creative School Leadership*. Perth: FORM.

Taplin, D. H. and Clark, H. (2012) *Theory of Change Basics: A Primer on Theory of Change*. New York: ActKnowledge. Available at: https://www.alnap.org/help-library/theory-of-change-basics-a-primer-on-theory-of-change.

Your reflection notes

Activity 11
Hang Out the Change Plan

🕐 1 hour

This activity might develop your creative habit of being ...

Wondering & questioning | **Tolerating uncertainty** **Daring to be different** | **Cooperating appropriately** **Giving & receiving feedback** | **Reflecting critically** | **Playing with possibilities**

Purpose

This activity follows the completion of your theory of change planning triangle and helps you to visualise the change by lifting it off the paper, allowing you to interact with it, notice where there might be gaps or where further detail might be useful. It also gives you the opportunity to begin to place the interventions along a timeline and, as leaders, to think about what actions you need to take and what resources you'll require along the way.

Resources and setting up

- White and coloured paper
- Marker pens
- Pegs and washing line or heavy-duty string
- Completed A3 theory of change planning triangles (from **Activity 10**)

Getting going

STEP 1 5 minutes

Begin by hanging the washing line or string across the room or tying it to two chairs a distance apart.

Write your final goals from your theory of change planning triangle on an item, or items, of clothing (drawn and cut from the paper) and peg them to the far right of your washing line. Do the same with your interventions, but this time peg them to the far left of the line.

Add your intermediate goals to the centre of the line.

Reflect together as a whole group and pose the following questions:

- Thinking about the washing line as a timeline, when does it start and when are we aiming to reach our final goals?

STEP 2 10 minutes

Once the group has reached a consensus, you may want to add some time periods or date markers to the washing line.

- How might you distribute the immediate goals and interventions along the timeline to begin creating an activity plan?

After you've rearranged the immediate goals and interventions, stand back and consider whether they're in the right sequence and if anything is missing and now needs to be added.

40 | Play 1 The Change Process

STEP 3 35 minutes

Split into three groups and assign each group to a different section of the washing line. Each group has 20 minutes to consider the interventions and/or goals in their section and add to the timeline using the following prompts:

- What leadership actions are essential to enable the changes, and when do they need to happen?
- Who else needs to be involved and when?
- What resources will be needed and when?

This should be done systematically, considering all the important steps and working backwards (right to left along the washing line) in the same way you created your theory of change. At the end of the 20 minutes, each group presents their section to everybody else. Allow some time for participants to add further contributions, remove repetitions or challenge the order of certain actions as you now look at the complete timeline.

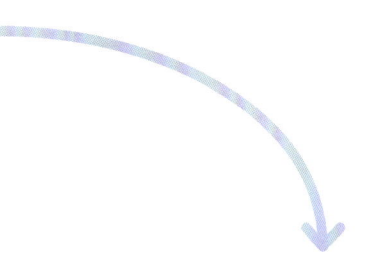

Reflecting together

STEP 4 10 minutes

- How has this activity helped your understanding of leading for creative thinking?
- Where can you foresee challenges along the timeline? How and when might you add some pre-emptive actions to mitigate these?
- How will this timeline be useful? What needs to happen to it next?

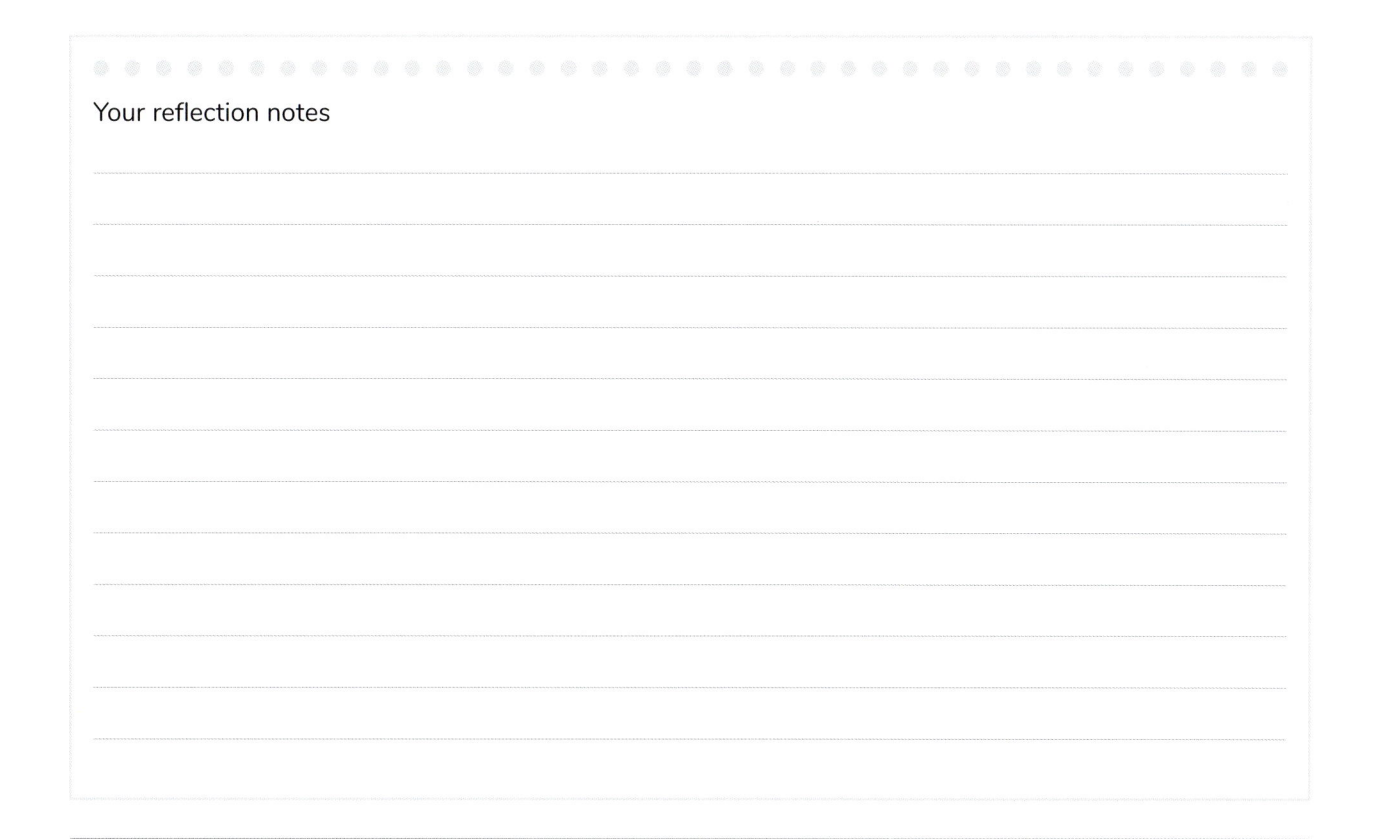

Your reflection notes

Activity 11 **Hang Out the Change Plan**

Activity 12
Develop Powerful Networks

🕐 1 hour 30 minutes

This activity might develop your creative habit of being . . .

Cooperating appropriately **Developing techniques** **Playing with possibilities / Making connections**

Purpose

Schools are networks of interconnected people. Through these connections, they develop relationships that help to build trust, move knowledge around and develop practice. Leaders have great opportunities to influence the ideas and behaviours of people in their networks and to learn from others. So, networks are powerful in spreading, supporting and extending change efforts. This activity helps you to think about your school(s) as social networks and identify your own professional social networks.

Resources and setting up

- TED Talk video by Nicholas Christakis: 'The Hidden Influence of Social Networks'[1]
- **Resource 12: Thinking About How Social Networks Can Support Educational Change**
- Large sheets of paper
- Jelly/gummy sweets (soft sweets that look like people)
- Paper clips
- Matches
- String
- Coloured dots/shapes
- Coloured pens
- Anything else you think might help you to create a network map (see **Resource 12**)
- Different-coloured sticky notes

Getting going

Take a moment to reiterate the purpose of this activity, recognising that, for some colleagues, the idea of knowledge being shared across networks may be a new one.

STEP 1 10 minutes

In groups of three to five, think about the professional relationships and networks you have that are focused on developing practice and enhancing pupil learning.

- What characterises the most powerful ones? Write these on sticky notes.
- What inhibits success? Write these on sticky notes of a different colour.

---

1 N. Christakis, The Hidden Influence of Social Networks [video]. *TED* (14 March 2014). Available at: https://www.ted.com/talks/nicholas_christakis_the_hidden_influence_of_social_networks?language=en.

42 | Play 1 **The Change Process**

STEP 2 20 minutes

Watch the TED Talk video.

STEP 3 10 minutes

Each group then writes their reflections on sticky notes and adds any additional characteristics.

Going deeper

STEP 4 15 minutes

Read **Resource 12**. As a group, come up with five key points you're taking from it.

STEP 5 20 minutes

Who is in your connections? Researchers use surveys to find out about social networks in schools. In this activity, you don't need to! Think about your connections; it may help to consider a change recently introduced in school.

Depending on your group size, create one or more maps of your group's social networks using your resources. Select particular colours or resources to represent different kinds of actors, connections, ties or specific activities.

Reflecting together

STEP 6 15 minutes

- What have you learned about your school(s) as a social network?
- Is it centralised or more distributed?
- How might you find out more about professional social networks in and beyond your school?
- What are the implications for leading for creative thinking in your school or across your schools?
- What will you do next?

Your reflection notes

Activity 13
Identify Challenges, Barriers and Uncertainties

1 hour 30 minutes

This activity might develop your creative habit of being ...

Challenging assumption | Tolerating uncertainty Sticking with difficulty | | Reflecting critically | Playing with possibilities

Purpose

This activity initially helps you to identify and think about barriers and challenges to leading and teaching for creativity. It'll help you and your team to voice the challenges and develop a shared understanding of the sorts of things you need to overcome together, and to think through possible resolutions. It could also be extended to involve broader participation from staff or across your wider networks of schools.

Resources and setting up

- Sufficient copies of **Resource 13: Common Change Challenges**, so it's visible to all participants working in small groups of three to six
- Room with tables for three to five people to provide a cafe atmosphere
- Each table to have paper tablecloth, flip chart paper and pens, coloured pens and coloured sticky dots

Getting going

STEP 1 20 minutes

On each table, look at the list of some of the reasons why people can resist change to promote creativity (**Resource 13**).

On flip chart paper, add your own challenges to this list.

At your table, decide on the top four to six challenges that you feel as a leader you can influence.

As a whole group, decide on the most significant of all these challenges. Each person has three coloured dots to use as votes for their challenges on the flip charts next to each table. Choose the top challenges according to the number of dots, limiting the total number selected to the number of tables.

44 | Play 1 **The Change Process**

Going deeper

STEP 2 40 minutes

Assign one challenge to each table and write the challenge prominently on the tablecloth. Talk about each challenge using brainstorming or a similar method to generate ideas. This will involve thinking about solutions to a shortlist of challenges in turn.

- Each table should spend five minutes writing their notes/thoughts on the tablecloth for the particular challenge.

- After five minutes, move to a different table and build on what is already there. Try not to duplicate what was written previously but come up with fresh insights/ideas.

- Once each group has visited all the tables, vote for what you feel are the most promising ideas in the room. You have six dots each – you can choose to use them all on one idea or distribute them across a number of ideas.

- Once the votes are counted, have a discussion on how to take the priority ideas forward.

Reflecting together

STEP 3 30 minutes

- As a leader, which of these solutions are you going to enact and when?

- How might you draw on your own creative habits of mind as you think about overcoming challenges?

- Which of these do you recognise as relevant in your situation?

- Think about your school and staff – which colleagues do you think are resistant to this change? What do you think their reasons are? They may be listed here or there may be other reasons.

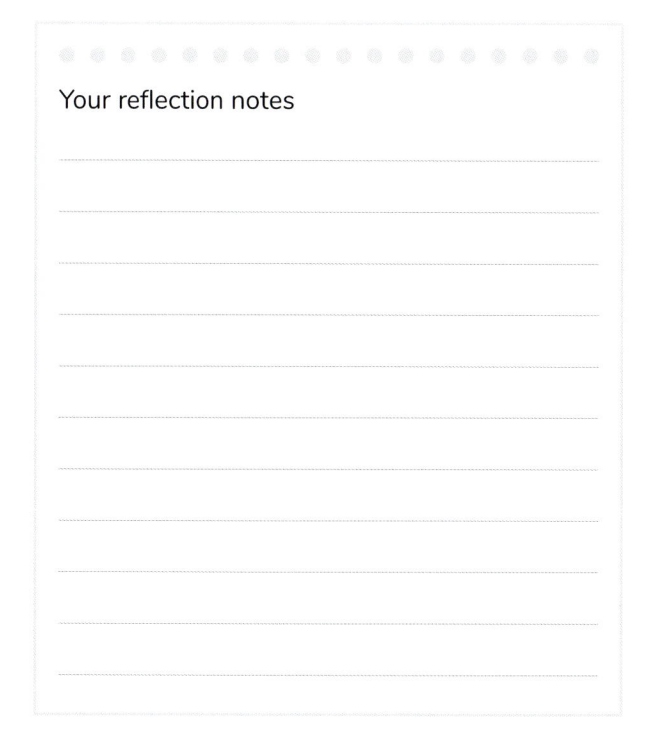

Your reflection notes

Activity 14
Mitigate Risks

1 hour 10 minutes

This activity might develop your creative habit of being …

Wondering & questioning
Challenging assumptions

Tolerating uncertainty
Sticking with difficulty
Daring to be different

Cooperating appropriately

Crafting & improving

Making connections
Playing with possibilities
Using intuition

Purpose

Developing leadership and teaching for creativity is hard and will inevitably raise issues along the way. This activity gives you an opportunity to consider the risks that may arise and explore possible ways to manage them. As the concept of risk can be very abstract, we've suggested a playful way of making them visible by using physical objects. You're invited to consider measures you might take in school or across your schools to assess the level of risk and the potential impact.

Resources and setting up

- Make sufficient copies of **Resource 14: Example Risk Matrix** for participants to have one each or to share in small groups

Getting going

STEP 1 — 40 minutes

Think about what your school might look like if things are going well in relation to the development of your learners' creative thinking habits of mind. What events might threaten this success? Examples might be:

- A change of staff/key staff leaving.
- Loss of momentum.
- Competing priorities.
- A drop in funding.
- A poor inspection report.

What would the (negative) consequence be?

For each consequence you wish to mitigate against, think about the likelihood and impact. The higher the likelihood and impact, the higher the risk. You might want to consider a simple three-part high–medium–low scale, like the one on page 47. You can replicate this on paper.

Play 1 **The Change Process**

High likelihood/low impact	High likelihood/medium impact	High likelihood/high impact *(High risk)*
Medium likelihood/low impact	Medium likelihood/medium impact	Medium likelihood/high impact
Low likelihood/low impact *(Low risk)*	Low likelihood/medium impact	Low likelihood/high impact

Or, you may want to use the template in **Resource 14** for a more granular approach.

Using **Resource 14**, you might identify the likelihood as 'likely' (scoring 4) and the impact as 'significant' (scoring 4). The associated risk score is 4 x 4 = 16, and the matrix is weighted to call this 'very high risk'. You may wish to play with the numbers to change which risk you call 'very low' and which you call 'extreme'. Plot each consequence in the blank template in **Resource 14**.

Going deeper

STEP 2 20 minutes

Now that you've put risks into the matrix, prioritise them from the most extreme to the very lowest risks.

Spend some time contingency planning, beginning with the highest priority risks. You can consider:

- Avoidance – what measures can you put in place to prevent the consequence(s) of the event (or even the event itself) from arising?
- Reduction – what steps can you take to reduce the impact of the event's consequence(s)?

Who else in your school could help you to think these things through?

Reflecting together

STEP 3 10 minutes

- Which are the most important risks to focus on?
- What contingency planning could mitigate the risks?
- What support would be helpful and from whom?
- How might the development of creative habits help to mitigate some of these risks?

Your reflection notes

Play 2
Develop Leaders

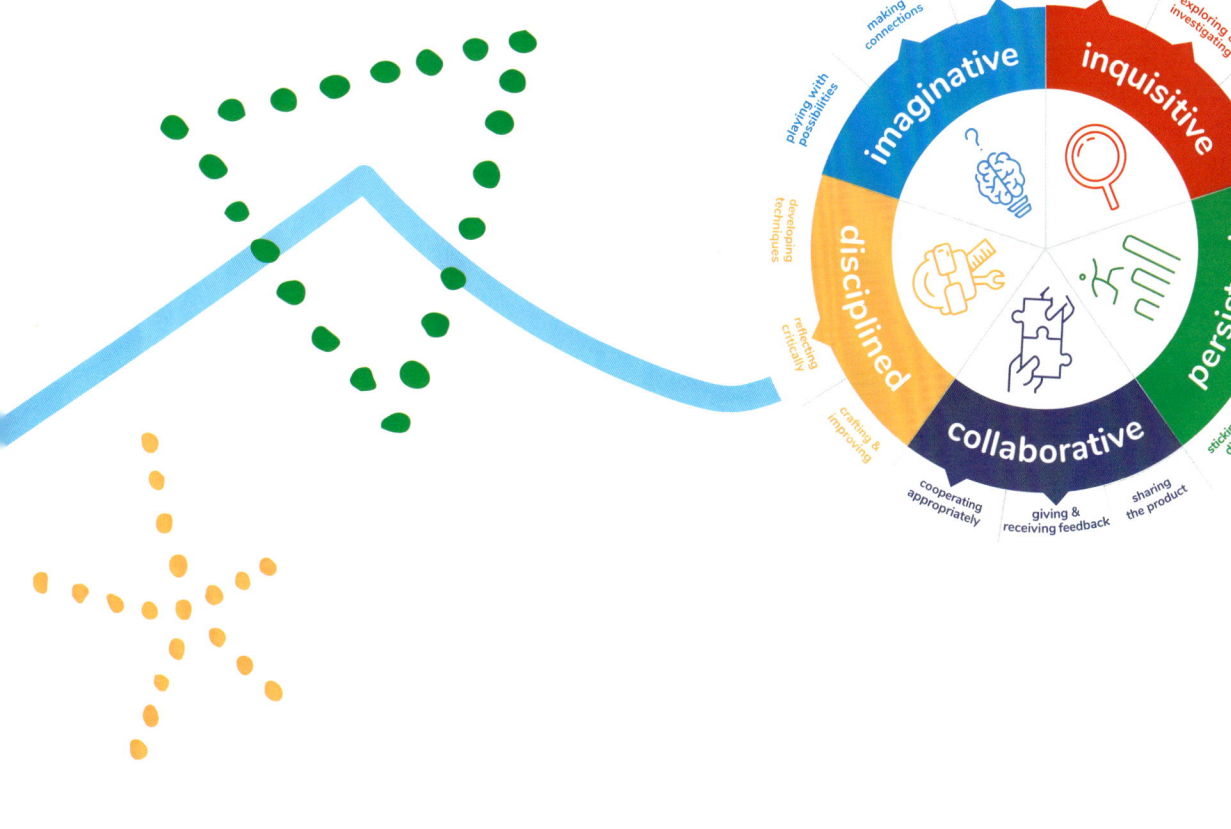

Activity 15
Identify, Enable and Grow Creative Change Catalysts

1 hour 10 minutes

This activity might develop your creative habit of being …

Exploring & investigating

Giving & receiving feedback

**Making connections
Playing with possibilities**

Purpose

Senior leaders create the culture that values and encourages the development of creative thinking, but they can't do it all when it comes to bringing about change related to teaching for creativity. They need to be able to distribute leadership to teacher leaders who play a role in leading change and enhancing pupil learning by influencing, co-developing and sharing professional knowledge and practice. This activity, for senior leadership teams in and across schools, supports you in identifying, enabling and growing creative change catalysts.

Resources and setting up

- **Resource 15:** Great Teacher Leader Characteristics
- **Resource 16:** The What and Who of Leadership
- **Resource 17:** Images for Identifying, Growing and Enabling Change Catalysts
- **Resource 18:** What Are You Doing? What Might You Do?

Getting going

STEP 1 10 minutes

Well-researched characteristics exist of teacher leaders who are catalysts who influence change and improvement in school.[1] Leading for creativity, however, is an emerging area when thinking about teacher leadership, with additional distinctive features.

Focusing on the yellow quadrant in **Resource 16**, as a group, first scan **Resource 15**, then talk about why the skills and qualities of creative change catalysts might be different.

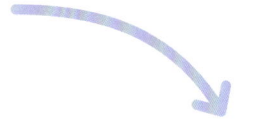

STEP 2 10 minutes

In your group, look at **Resource 17**. Select images that resonate when you think of the characteristics of teacher leaders who are creative change catalysts.

---

1 See L. Stoll, C. Taylor, K. Spence-Thomas and C. Brown, *Catalyst: An Evidence-Informed Collaborative, Professional Learning Resource for Teacher Leaders and Other Leaders Working in and Across Schools* (Carmarthen: Crown House Publishing, 2021).

50 | Play 2 **Develop Leaders**

STEP 3 15 minutes

Drawing on our recent experiences with those leading creative thinking in schools internationally and combining this with our knowledge from research, here are some of the emerging common characteristics of creative change catalysts:

- Recognising creativity in colleagues.
- Valuing creativity in colleagues.
- Being courageous/brave.
- Risk-taking.
- Curiosity.

How do these characteristics compare with yours? What is the same or similar? What is different? Drawing on your earlier conversations and the images, review and add to the list of characteristics.

STEP 4 10 minutes

Take a characteristic and describe concrete examples of teachers in your school(s) who demonstrate this, or what you would expect to see and hear. Repeat this for some other characteristics.

Going deeper

STEP 5 10 minutes

Use **Resource 18** to consider and capture what you're already doing and what (else) you might do to develop, enable and support creative change catalysts.

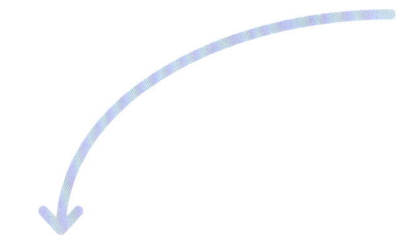

Reflecting together

STEP 6 15 minutes

- What are your key learnings from this activity?
- Did anything surprise or challenge you?
- What factors might potentially inhibit potential creative change catalysts in your school, and what might you do about this?
- What kind of inquiry might you carry out to find out more about creative change catalysts and how to identify, develop and support them?
- What are your priorities moving forward?

Your reflection notes

Activity 15 **Identify, Enable and Grow Creative Change Catalysts**

Play 3
Change the Culture

Activity 16
Core Values to Support Creativity

See below

This activity might develop your creative habit of being ...

inquisitive — Wondering & questioning, Exploring & investigating

persistent

collaborative — Giving & receiving feedback

disciplined — Reflecting critically

imaginative — Making connections

Purpose

This whole-staff activity will help you to think through how the school's core values support the development of creativity. It's designed to help you consider and seek out evidence of where core values link to creativity. You'll have the opportunity to interrogate and justify the evidence, also thinking about opportunities to develop (further) links between core values and creativity.

Duration

This activity would work well as part of a whole-school development day as it takes more than 1 hour 30 minutes. It might also be good to consider alongside **Activity 6: Be Clear About the Purpose of School**, which also looks at vision and mission statements. In this current activity you'll be focusing on your school's more detailed set of values/ethos/core principles.

As you reflect on values that might conflict with creativity, this could link to **Activity 13: Identify Challenges, Barriers and Uncertainties**.

Resources and setting up

This guide works through the activity for a group of 15–30 participants. Adapt accordingly for more or fewer colleagues.

Numbered tables:

- Sufficient for three to six participants to gather around each table (fewer is preferable).

For each table:

- Two copies of the school's values (ethos/core principles) on A4 paper, with values separated and spaced evenly down the page.
- One copy of **Resource 1: Five Creative Habits Framework** for reference.
- Two different sheets from **Resource 4: Creative Individuals Are ...** There are five different resource sheets, one for each of the five creative habits. Print twice as many as the number of tables so that each table has two different ones.
- Two pieces of large paper/chart paper.
- Glue or tape for sticking paper.
- Felt pens/marker pens, pencils and a long ruler.

54 | Play 3 **Change the Culture**

For whole-group activity:

- Wall or whiteboard space.
- Single large copy of the school's values.
- Single large copy of **Resource 2: Descriptions of the Creative Habits**.
- Multiple copies of **Resource 19: Evidence Sheet** – each table might need five to 10.

The whole-group element could be done using collaborative software instead which would allow groups to post text and images.

Set up each of the tables to include two pieces of large paper oriented landscape, a copy of the school's values (stuck on the left) and a copy of one of the five sheets from **Resource 4** (stuck on the right) as below. Place a single copy of **Resource 1** on each table.

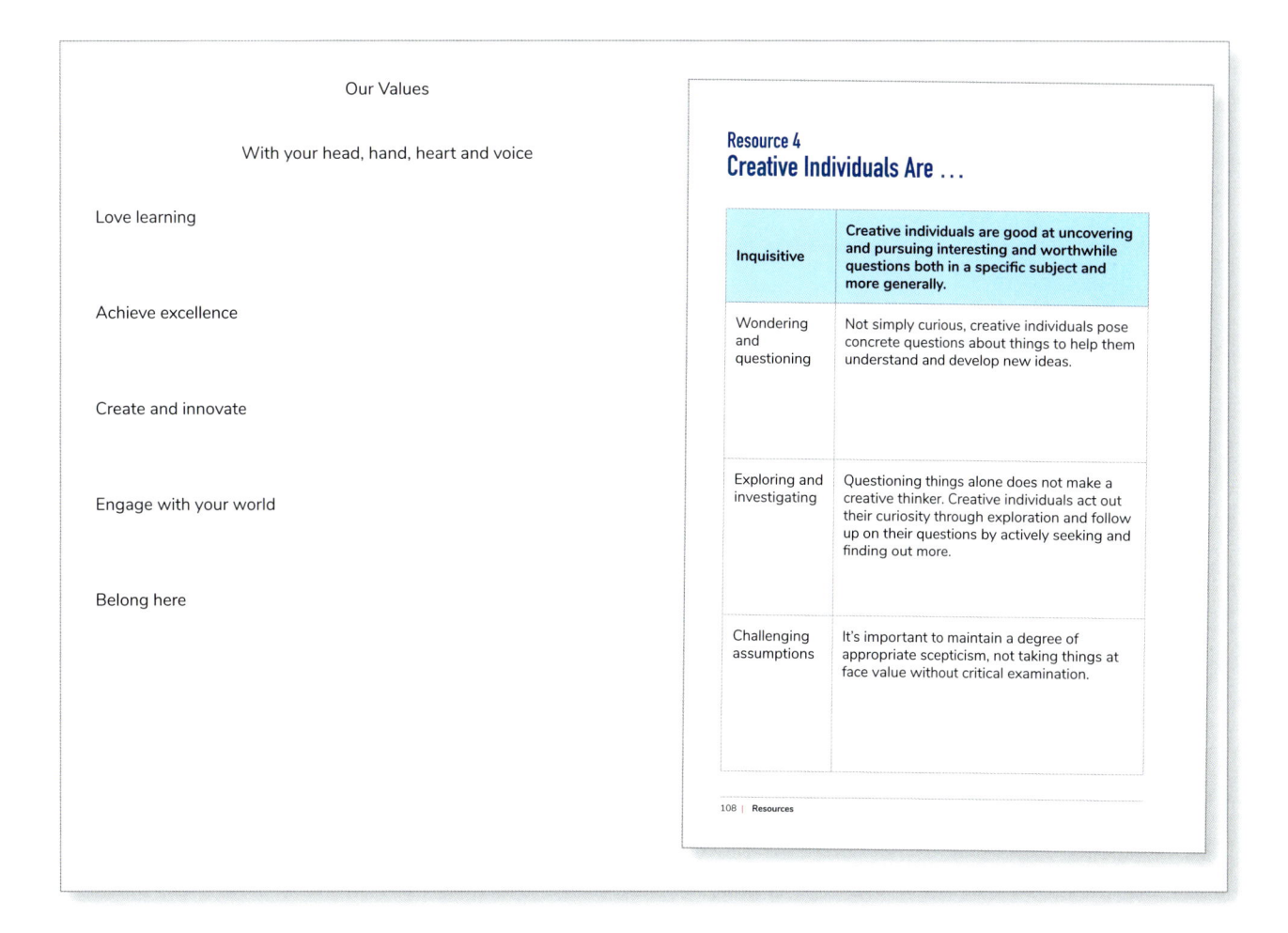

Our Values

With your head, hand, heart and voice

- Love learning
- Achieve excellence
- Create and innovate
- Engage with your world
- Belong here

Resource 4
Creative Individuals Are …

Inquisitive	**Creative individuals are good at uncovering and pursuing interesting and worthwhile questions both in a specific subject and more generally.**
Wondering and questioning	Not simply curious, creative individuals pose concrete questions about things to help them understand and develop new ideas.
Exploring and investigating	Questioning things alone does not make a creative thinker. Creative individuals act out their curiosity through exploration and follow up on their questions by actively seeking and finding out more.
Challenging assumptions	It's important to maintain a degree of appropriate scepticism, not taking things at face value without critical examination.

Assign resource sheets to each group to give different combinations – for example, collaborative and disciplined, disciplined and imaginative, imaginative and inquisitive, inquisitive and persistent, persistent and collaborative. Each group will look at two habits alongside the school's values.

On a visible wall or large board, reproduce this layout, with a large copy of the school's values on the left like in the example below from Eleanor Palmer Primary School in Camden:

Our Values

With your head, hand, heart and voice

Love learning

Achieve excellence

Create and innovate

Engage with your world

Belong here

Resource 2
Descriptions of the Creative Habits

Inquisitive	Creative individuals are good at uncovering and pursuing interesting and worthwhile questions both in a specific subject and more generally.
Wondering and questioning	Not simply curious, creative individuals pose concrete questions about things to help them understand and develop new ideas.
Exploring and investigating	Questioning things alone does not make a creative thinker. Creative individuals act out their curiosity through exploration and follow up on their questions by actively seeking and finding out more.
Challenging assumptions	It's important to maintain a degree of appropriate scepticism, not taking things at face value without critical examination.
Persistent	Creative individuals don't give up easily.
Tolerating uncertainty	Being able to tolerate uncertainty is important when actions or even goals aren't fully set out.
Sticking with difficulty	Persistence in the form of tenacity is important, enabling an individual to get beyond familiar ideas and come up with new ones.

Getting going

STEP 1 10 minutes for introduction and reading

Creativity is more likely to thrive when supported by a school's core values, and certainly when not in conflict with them.

Make sure everyone is clear about the broad process that follows before you start – that is, during the session you'll first need to find connections between the school's values and habits of mind, and cite evidence, before searching for photographic evidence.

Participants divide into groups of three to six per table. Each table will focus on two of the five habits. Everyone first reads **Resource 2**. Each table selects a scribe and considers their school's values in turn.

Play 3 **Change the Culture**

STEP 2 10 minutes for each sub-habit

1. How does this habit/sub-habit fit with the values? If a value connects to one of the three creativity sub-habits on the first sheet, draw a clear line between the two, highlight it with a brightly coloured pen or indicate the connection clearly.

2. For each link, what in the school demonstrates this value and habit? What photographic (or other) evidence could we collect? For example, pupils might spend time out in the community gardening each week, which links to the school's value of 'improving our community' and helps with the sub-habit of 'crafting and improving'. Visual evidence from around the school will be used to endorse that the school values support this habit and its sub-elements.

Agree as a whole group how the scribes will write down the evidence idea (e.g. on a sticky note or in a colour-coded box).

The scribe writes sufficient notes to enable another group to understand what the link is and the proposed evidence.

3. Repeat this process for each of the school's values with the second habit.

4. In the next step, each group's work is evaluated and challenged by colleagues. First, write your table number on your sheets. Swap each of the two habits you've worked on with tables working on the same habit. You might choose to do this once or twice, depending on the number of tables and how much time you have. For each round, each table explores what colleagues at other tables have come up with when thinking about the same habits.

Going deeper

STEP 3 At least 15 minutes

5. The sheets are returned to their original tables. Colleagues then come to a consensus about which values link to which habits, about the best ideas for evidence collection and how they will collect evidence. Various options are possible for evidence collection. You might wish to pick a colour for each habit, and each group identifies 10 forms of evidence across the five habits and sticks them on the wall next to the relevant school value.

6. Taking each value in turn, contributors explain their choice of evidence. Where multiple forms of evidence are suggested from various tables, groups might pose questions to one another and vote for the best form(s) of evidence.

STEP 4 20 minutes

7. Once agreed upon, each table will collect evidence for their two habits via a photographic 'field trip' around the school using mobile devices. Your group might want to use **Resource 19** to record more information and then hold the sheet in front of the camera while taking pictures to make sure it's clear which habit the evidence supports. The best photographs are then selected (agree on an upper limit) and sent to print or collated on an electronic version of the whiteboard/wall display.

STEP 5 20 minutes

8. Everybody comments on the photos, particularly where a habit/sub-habit–value link has more than one form of evidence. This central version is now a distillation of the best ideas and evidence. It should be recorded and updated, and can form the basis of dialogue about school values.

Reflecting together

STEP 6 20 minutes

- Which of your values support creativity? Are there any that might offer greater support?
- Are there any values that might conflict with creativity?
- Where you think there are links, could you evidence this better and what would you need to do differently to provide such evidence more readily?
- What other non-photographic evidence do you need to consider?

Your reflection notes

Activity 17
Develop a Common Language

1 hour 10 minutes

This activity might develop your creative habit of being . . .

Exploring & investigating
Challenging assumptions

Daring to be different

Purpose

Language is vitally important in supporting a culture where teachers are empowered and enabled to lead change. Leaders can powerfully influence language in schools. This activity is designed to help you think about the language you use and to develop a common language that lives and breathes the creative habits of mind. It'll also support and strengthen a democratic process of change for teaching for creativity.

Resources and setting up

- Copies of a variety of different communication materials produced by the school
- A black marker pen for each participant
- A copy of **Resource 1: Five Creative Habits Framework**

This activity is initially for senior leaders and could take place over time as you consider different aspects of language in your school. Alongside developing a common language, leaders have a critical role in ensuring that the language and words used are understood by the whole school community and become part of the everyday life of the school. Therefore, you'll want to involve staff and pupils in these conversations as you move along.

Getting going

Begin by reading **Resource 20: The Power of Language**.

STEP 1 15 minutes

You can choose to do this part either as an observation before the conversation or going straight into reflection together (the suggested timing is for the latter). You may wish to do this as a whole group or break into smaller groups, each focusing on a different point.

- What words or phrases would an observer of your last senior leadership team meeting have heard?
- What words or phrases would a visitor to your last three assemblies have heard?
- What words or phrases would a fly on the wall in your last couple of staff meetings have heard?
- What words or phrases would a visitor hear if observing one of your best teachers?
- What different words or phrases would a visitor hear if observing one of your other teachers?

Having considered these questions, now think about what messages these convey to the receiver. How do these words and messages embody the creative habits and engage others in taking this forward throughout the school?

Activity 17 **Develop a Common Language** | 59

Going deeper

STEP 2 25 minutes

For this 'creativity blackout' activity, work in small groups, each looking at a different source of written material produced by the school to highlight where the habits of mind are present. You could include:

- Recent newsletters, including those written by leaders, staff and pupils.
- Correspondence from leadership to staff, pupils and parents.
- A range of pupil report cards.
- Papers for governors/boards of management/trustee meetings.
- Print-outs from the school website.

Each participant takes their source material, a copy of **Resource 1** and a marker pen. Begin by circling all the words, sentences or phrases that align with the habits. Then black out the rest of the text on the page, the result of which is a creativity blackout (as in the example below).

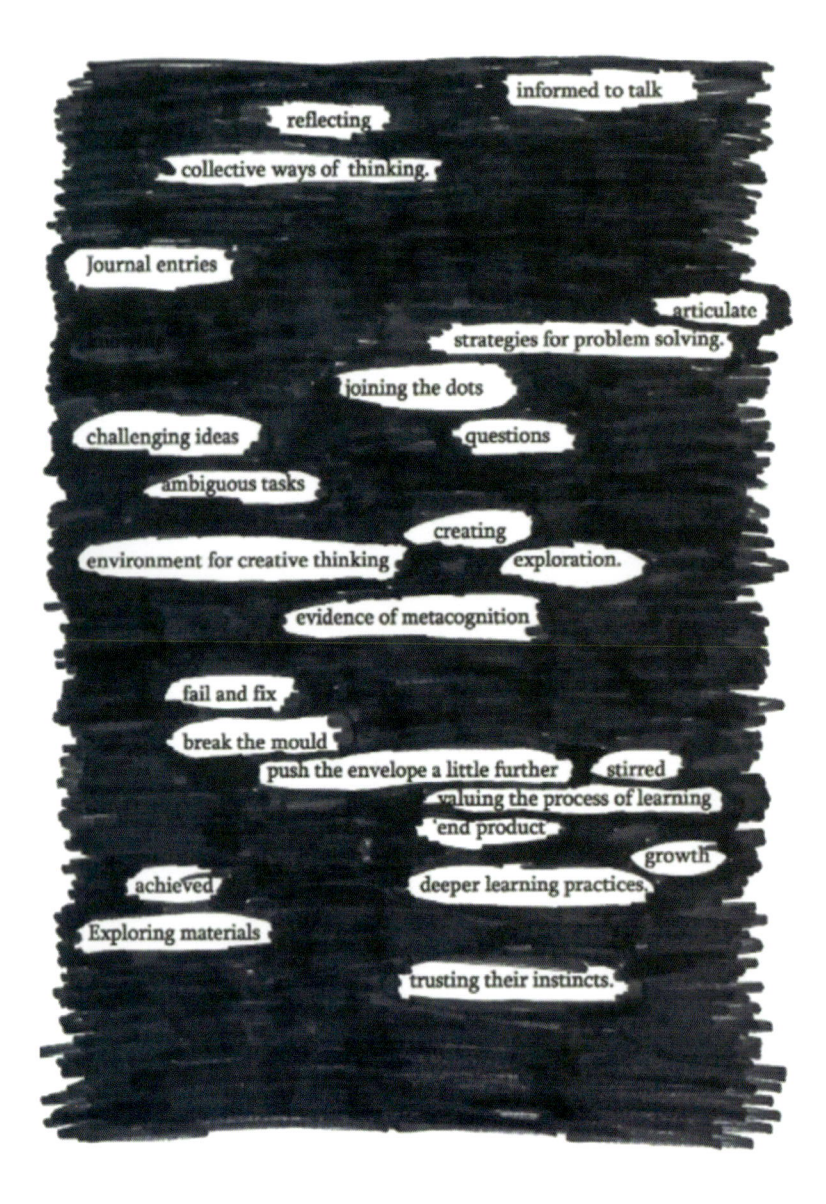

- Where are you seeing creativity most in your school's communication?
- Where are you noticing it least?

60 | Play 3 **Change the Culture**

STEP 3 15 minutes

The formal and informal language used around school more generally is important in creating the conditions whereby staff feel more motivated to change. From Louise Stoll's previous work, we find that words and phrases that are more likely to engage colleagues in change share certain characteristics, which are shown on the left-hand side of the table below.[1]

Words/phrases that are:	Rather than:
Active	Passive
Adaptive	Prescriptive
Empowering	Constraining
Oriented collectively	Oriented individually
Inclusive	Exclusive
Multidirectional	One-way

From the words and phrases generated in the 'getting going' activity on page 59, which ones align with those on the left-hand side of the table and which with the right? Which words or phrases from your 'getting going' list might it be valuable to change to develop your language as a creative school?

Reflecting together

STEP 4 15 minutes

- What surprised you about the language used in your school?
- How do you develop an understanding of the language of and for creativity?
- What are you already doing, and what do you need to do, to change the language in your school to support creative thinking?
- What are your next steps?
- How will you evaluate the progress you're making?
- How could you use this activity or adapt it for staff?

Your reflection notes

---

1 L. Stoll, *Language for Learning Leadership*. Occasional Paper 167 (Melbourne, VIC: Centre for Strategic Education, 2020). Available at: https://discovery.ucl.ac.uk/id/eprint/10109744.

Activity 18
Debunk Myths About Creativity

🕐 1 hour 10 minutes

This activity might develop your creative habit of being ...

inquisitive — *persistent* **Sticking with difficulty / Daring to be different** — *collaborative* — *disciplined* **Crafting & improving** — *imaginative*

Purpose

Besides being clearer about what creativity is, creative leaders need to be aware of a number of myths they may encounter. This activity helps you to deepen your understanding of creativity, build your confidence in articulating accessible definitions or descriptions of it, and exercise leadership in countering some of the myths that still hinder the development of young people's creativity.

Resources and setting up

- **Resource 21: Five Myths About Creativity**
- Six index cards, or similar, for each small group
- Flip chart paper
- Marker pens

Getting going

STEP 1 15 minutes

Your beliefs about what it is to be creative strongly shape the way you see yourselves and others. To take an extreme view to make the point, if you thought that only girls could be really creative, then each time you taught a mixed class you would be prejudiced against the likelihood of a boy demonstrating their creative thinking!

In small groups, make a list of three things you believe to be true about creativity. Write these on the cards and turn them face down. Then come up with three things you've heard someone saying that you *don't* believe to be true. Share all the cards and shuffle the 'pack'.

Make three columns on a flip chart, headed 'Truths', 'Myths' and 'Don't know'. As one person now turns over each card, agree which of the statements are false, which are true and which you're uncertain about. Write them down under the relevant column.

If you want to get up on your feet for this, use the method we introduced in the 'getting going' section of **An example activity** on page 3.

62 | Play 3 **Change the Culture**

Going deeper

STEP 2 15 minutes

Getting your head around the arguments. Read the five myths about creativity in **Resource 21**. These are five of the many ideas about creativity that can be particularly undermining for any school leader trying to work with staff.

Split into five groups and each take one of these myths. For each one, make a list of other points you would want to stress. Use the playbook and any of the resources you have to hand to help you.

STEP 3 30 minutes

Dealing with sceptics. Every staffroom has them. Sometimes they just don't like change, sometimes they believe it isn't part of their educational philosophy, but often someone can take against a possible change because they don't understand it or have been influenced by others to see it as unhelpful. While leaders can't always convince a sceptic, it's worth having a try. This role play will help you to prepare for sceptics at the same time as it builds your understanding.

In pairs, take one of the myths. The person playing the sceptic starts by using a version of the myth as an objection to the idea of creativity. The other responds with an 'elevator pitch' (a short, well-argued statement) to try and persuade them of an alternative point of view.

When everyone has had a go, come together as a whole group, listen to some examples and take it in turns to come up with persuasive pitches, giving each other suggestions along the way.

Reflecting together

STEP 4 10 minutes

- Which of these five myths do you find most difficult to debunk?
- In your school, which myth is most prevalent, and what could you do at a whole-school level to debunk it?

Your reflection notes

Play 4
Rethink Structures

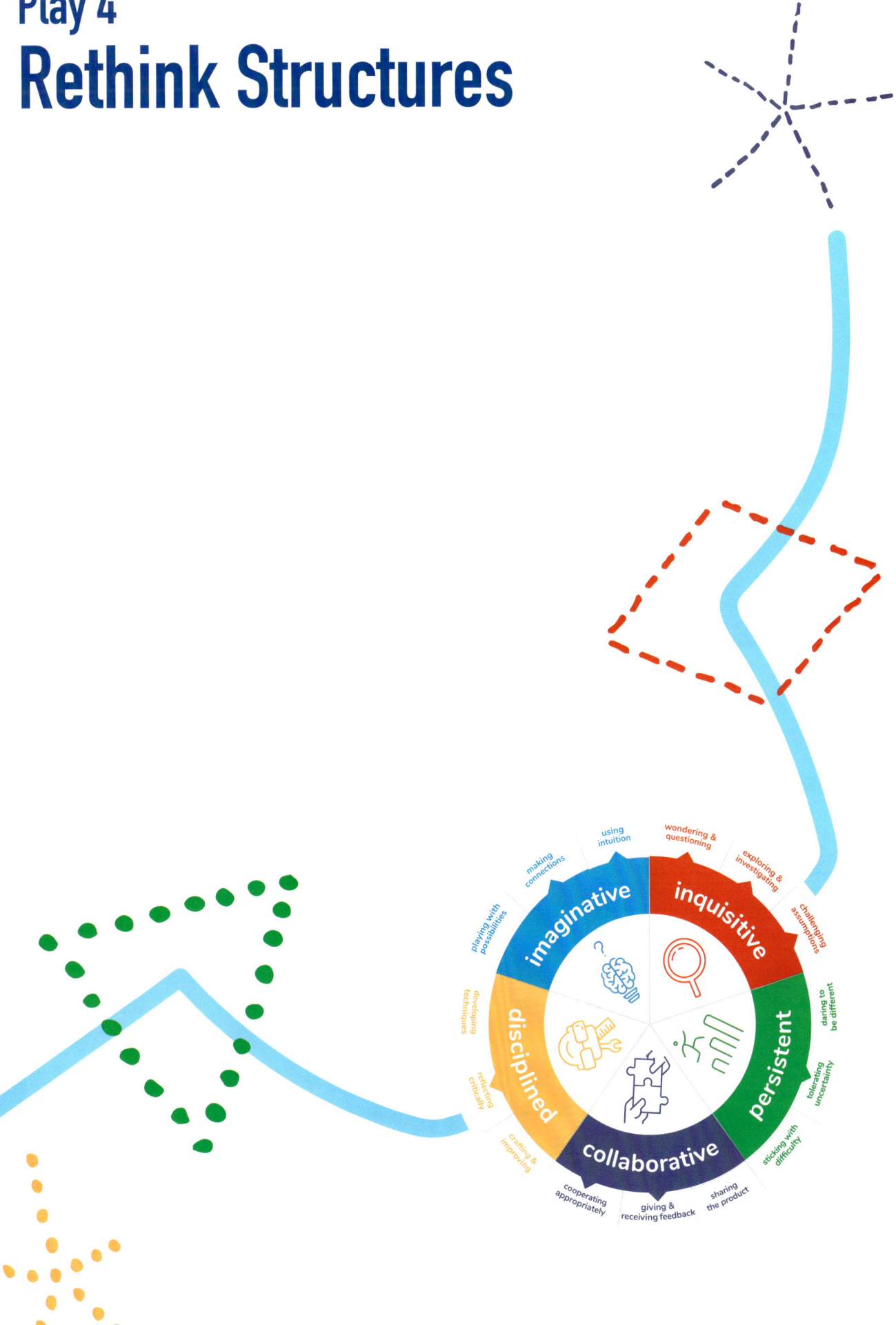

Activity 19
Thread It Through the School Improvement Plan

1 hour

This activity might develop your creative habit of being ...

Exploring & investigating | | | Reflecting critically | Making connections

Purpose

When you're intentional about planning for and developing creativity within existing documents and mechanisms within school, including the school improvement plan, it can have a significant impact on successful outcomes. This activity invites you to consider your current school improvement plan/school development plan and review how many areas relate to improving creativity and whether there's room for further development.

Resources and setting up

- Your school improvement plan/school development plan
- Pens
- Red, orange and green pens or sticky dots

Getting going

STEP 1 45 minutes

Use your school's development plan and the areas within it to analyse the progress of creativity being made across the school. Use the red, amber, green rating to reflect on where things are going well and where there are opportunities for improvement – for example:

- Professional learning
- Curriculum
- Communications
- Partnerships
- Collaboration
- Leadership
- Pupil voice
- Wellbeing

Here are some questions that may help your discussions:

- What makes you say those areas are red, amber or green?
- What is enabling those areas of creativity?
- Where are there opportunities to improve?

Reflecting together

STEP 2 15 minutes

- Looking at your responses, can you agree on five key next steps to explore further?
- How will you put these into action?
- As creative leaders, how will you ensure all staff are invested in this?

66 | Play 4 **Rethink Structures**

Activity 20
Reimagine Systems

1 hour

This activity might develop your creative habit of being …

- **Wondering & questioning** (inquisitive)
- **Daring to be different** (persistent)
- **Cooperating appropriately** (collaborative)
- **Reflecting critically** (disciplined)
- **Playing with possibilities / Using intuition** (imaginative)

Purpose

Creative leadership requires looking at the bigger picture. It's impossible to create meaningful and impactful change by tinkering with aspects of the current system only, when these instruments are themselves influenced by or designed to serve the system! This activity is for you as leaders to explore your school policies, structures, resources and practices, and reimagine how they could be adapted to enable and provoke creative thinking.

Resources and setting up

- A3 paper (landscape) cut into thirds to create strips
- Pens
- Arrange chairs in a circle before the participants arrive

Getting going

STEP 1 · 10 minutes

Start with participants sitting in a circle with a strip of paper and a pen in hand. Invite everyone to think about the policies, structures, resources and practices that are needed to keep any school operational and effective – for example:

Policies	Structures	Resources	Practices
Appraisal or performance management Human resources	Faculty/department/age–phase organisation	Time	Staff meetings

As a group, think about your own examples to add to those listed above and write them on your strips of paper. Lay the strips on the floor in the middle of the circle in a sundial formation.

STEP 2 20 minutes

Consider whether each of the elements on the strips is currently more likely to be enabling or inhibiting teaching for creativity. To do this, each person in the circle looks at the nearest two or three strips of paper in front of them and considers whether those policies, structures, resources or practices, and the way they're currently set up, support creativity.

Going deeper

STEP 3 20 minutes

Now that you've considered what *is*, you're going to think about what *could be*. Use your imagination to think differently about your policies, structures, resources and practices. How could they be better used, designed and planned for to ensure they both provoke and sustain the best conditions for teaching for creativity?

- How can faculty/department/phase leaders rethink the appraisal process?
- Where might you be able to free up time for professional learning?
- How could staff meetings be reconfigured to stimulate cross-curricular planning?

Rather than going around the circle, anyone can offer a suggestion at any time by starting their response with, 'I wonder if ...'

Reflecting together

STEP 4 10 minutes

- What has this activity brought into focus for you?
- What are the easy wins, and what can you act on immediately?
- What are longer-term aims, and what actions do you need to take to reach them?
- What might you need to investigate further before taking action?
- Acting on some of the outcomes from the possibility thinking exercise will require you to take some risks. How does this make you feel?

Your reflection notes

Play 5
Develop a Creative Curriculum

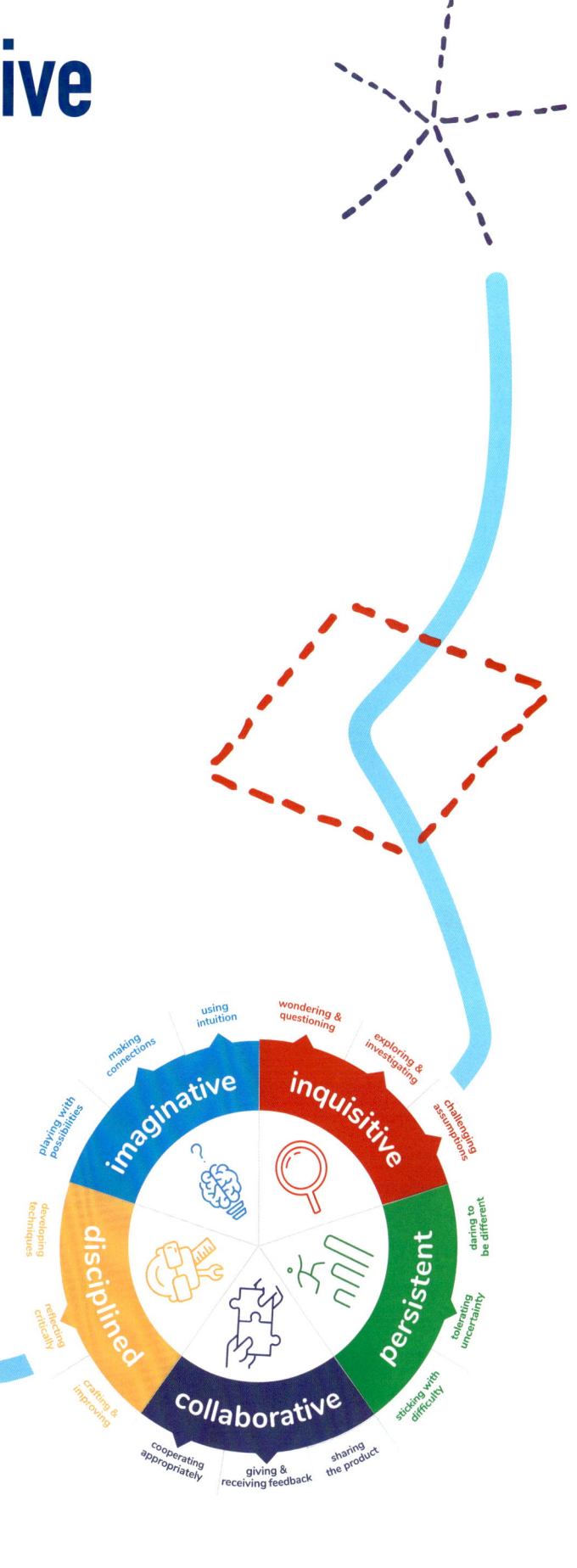

Activity 21
Embed Creativity in the Curriculum

1 hour
15 minutes

This activity might develop your creative habit of being ...

Challenging assumptions (inquisitive) — **persistent** — **collaborative** — **Crafting & improving / Reflecting critically** (disciplined) — **Playing with possibilities** (imaginative)

Purpose

Embedding creativity in every subject of the school curriculum requires an understanding of the potential of every discipline. This activity invites you to talk with curriculum leads to develop your understanding of how the school can intentionally plan for creativity throughout the curriculum. It encourages you to map the creative habits against your curriculum to enable more opportunities for creativity and critical thinking. This activity is a stimulus, which you can use at any stage, develop further or check in with at a later date.

Resources and setting up

- Your chosen curriculum area's curriculum lead (invite one lead per creative leader present)
- Relevant national curriculum documents
- Relevant longer-term school curriculum planning documents
- Copies of the five sheets from **Resource 4: Creative Individuals Are ...** which detail the creative habits of mind and their sub-habits
- Sticky dots or highlighter pens matched to each of the five creative habits of mind to map against the curriculum
- Access to Alberta's helpful mapping of creative thinking (and other competences) to different subjects in the curriculum: https://education.alberta.ca/competencies/competencies-in-subjects

Getting going

In this activity, you'll map the five creative habits against specific subject curricula to enable more opportunities for creativity and critical thinking.

STEP 1 20 minutes

In groups, look at your curriculum documents and **Resource 4** and discuss in your groups where and how are they aligned.

Use the coloured pens or sticky dots in your five chosen colours to mark where you see the habits and their sub-habits potentially being developed within the curriculum.

Now work through the same documents considering where and how the five habits could be developed further.

- What opportunities could you build on?
- What opportunities might you be missing?
- Where are there opportunities for the creative habits to be further integrated into the planning and design of your curriculum?
- How could the creative habits be more visible, and what could you do more of?

Once you've explored where the habits are aligned with this area of the curriculum and where there may be further opportunities to develop these, share what you've noticed.

Play 5 **Develop a Creative Curriculum**

Going deeper

STEP 2 40 minutes

As a school leader, how can you ensure that the learning that has just occurred – the mapping of creative habits against curriculum content – can be used in practice across the school?

We introduced the idea of split screen teaching earlier (see **Activity 8**), explaining that it invites teachers to describe two worlds: the disciplinary subject matter of their lesson *and* the creative habit on which they're also focusing. Use the idea of split screen planning and teaching to help you here.

Let's say you were introducing a science activity to understand the properties of acids and bases, and then preparing a short demonstration for other pupils who, in turn, will offer feedback to their peers on the effectiveness of their explanations. In the imaginary split screen of the lesson and its objectives, a teacher would take care to explain to the class that both the chemistry (acids and bases) and the creative thinking (giving and receiving feedback) objectives were equally important.

Use this approach to invite colleagues to plan, first, a series of lessons, then a term's work and finally a whole year of creative thinking in their subject. Use flip chart sheets or digital equivalents to capture and share this with the group.

Reflecting together

STEP 3 15 minutes

- What are you already doing that you can build on?
- How can you as a leader ensure that these practices are shared?
- How can you do this systematically and intentionally?
- How can you adapt your existing curriculum planning documents to make split screen planning central to the life of the school?
- How can you create time for this kind of planning to take place routinely among staff?

Your reflection notes

Activity 21 **Embed Creativity in the Curriculum** | 71

Activity 22
Look Beyond the Classroom

🕐 1 hour

This activity might develop your creative habit of being ...

inquisitive — Wondering & questioning, Exploring & investigating, Challenging assumptions

persistent

collaborative

disciplined — Developing techniques, Reflecting critically

imaginative — Making connections, Playing with possibilities

Purpose

Creativity can be taught and learned through a range of informal, extra-curricular activities and by working in partnership with others from a range of sectors. This activity invites you to consider creativity in areas of the school not related to subjects. It could also involve assemblies, visiting speakers or tutor group activities.

Resources and setting up

- Any materials describing the extra-curricular activities your school runs
- Copies of **Resource 22: Thinking About Your Locality**

Getting going

STEP 1 20 minutes

In pairs, take a moment to think about how you might develop pupils' creativity outside the classroom, whether nearby in your school grounds or further afield. Share your ideas. What are you already doing? Which organisations do you already have relationships with that might help? Which of the creative habits have been nurtured from these habits? Share your discussions.

Reflecting together

STEP 3 10 minutes

- What simple changes could you initiate to enrich the creative content of pupils' extra-curricular life?
- When you think of individual year groups, how many informal opportunities to develop creativity are you offering them?
- How could you plan creative opportunities for pupils beyond the formal curriculum more systematically and strategically?

Going deeper

STEP 2 30 minutes

In groups of four to six, look at **Resource 22**. Use this chart to prompt you to think about the following:

- What are you already doing that encourages creativity outside the formal curriculum?
- How could this be developed further?
- Which of the ideas on the chart have helped you to think of new ideas, and what are they?
- How could you map the creative habits against extra-curricular activities?

72 | Play 5 **Develop a Creative Curriculum**

Play 6
Rethink Pedagogy

Activity 23
Use Signature Pedagogies for Creativity

1 hour 15 minutes

This activity might develop your creative habit of being ...

inquisitive   *persistent*   *collaborative*   *disciplined*   *imaginative*

Developing techniques
Reflecting critically

Purpose

The choices staff make in the classroom about teaching and learning really matter. This activity explores the idea of signature pedagogies – that there are some methods that are most likely to cultivate pupils' creativity (and their own). It invites you to think about how you can grow teachers' confidence in choosing and using a full repertoire of pedagogies that will promote creative thinking.

Resources and setting up

- A copy of **Resource 23: Signature Pedagogies for Creative Thinking** for each small group

Getting going

STEP 1   20 minutes

If you wanted to teach a pupil how to become more imaginative and better able to play with possibilities, what methods would you choose? What if you wanted pupils to become more inquisitive and better able to challenge assumptions? Or, if your intention was to encourage pupils to stick with uncertainty, give and receive feedback or reflect critically, how would you select the most appropriate pedagogy?

It's helpful for teachers to use the idea of signature pedagogies when considering these questions. A signature pedagogy is a teaching and learning method specifically designed with a particular learning outcome in mind – in this case, the development of an aspect of creative thinking. Think of 'signature' as in a 'signature dish'; the recipe most associated with a particular chef.

In groups, look at **Resource 23**. For each of the five creative habits, we've identified a signature pedagogy with three examples of teaching and learning methods linked to a specific aspect of the habit. For example, problem-based learning is the overall name for a family of approaches likely to encourage inquisitive learning and includes techniques such as Philosophy for Children.

Which of these are you familiar with? How widely are these approaches used in your school(s)?

Going deeper

STEP 2 45 minutes

To help your colleagues develop a repertoire of pedagogies, it's helpful to think about, first of all, how you as a teacher would go about selecting pedagogies that are appropriate for the desired creative habit, subject context (maths, science, geography, etc.) and age of the pupils.

Your own understanding: In pairs, take a sub-habit, choose a subject and a specific unit of work, and select a class of pupils you know. Plan an imaginary lesson together and share this with another pair.

Developing staff practice: In the same pairs, plan a series of professional learning sessions to build the confidence of your colleagues. This might include:

- Asking colleagues to annotate an A3 size version of **Resource 23** to show which pedagogies they're currently using.
- Over a half-term, taking the opportunity to get different teachers to take five minutes in a staff briefing session to introduce a method such as Mantle of the Expert, thinking routines or jigsaw.
- Creating opportunities for staff to observe each other in action.
- Scheduling professional learning sessions focusing on a particular signature pedagogy.

Think about these suggestions and add your own. Come back together as a whole group and share your ideas.

Reflecting together

STEP 3 10 minutes

- What is your school already doing well?
- Where are colleagues least confident, and why do you think this is?
- How can you support those colleagues who find changing their teaching methods most challenging?

Your reflection notes

Play 7
Track Progression in Creative Thinking

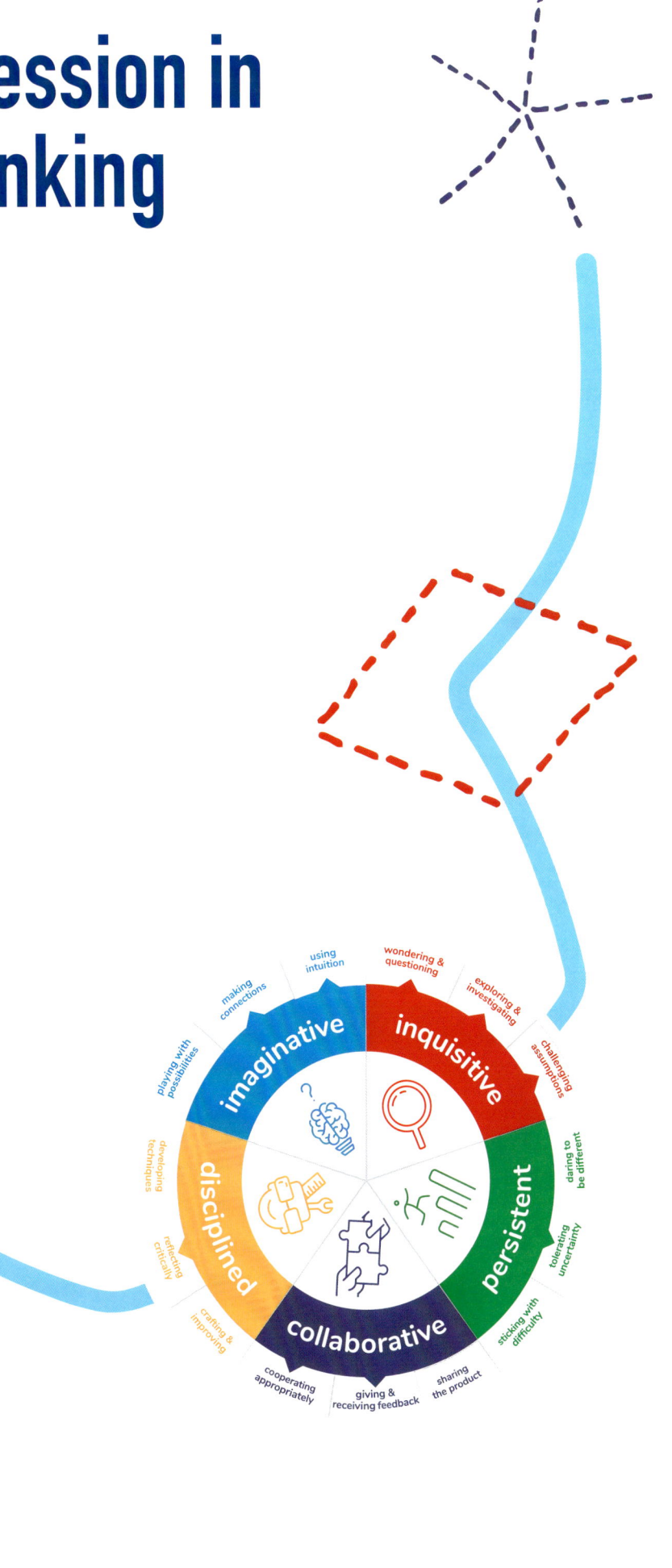

Activity 24
Rethink Assessment

1 hour

This activity might develop your creative habit of being ...

Reflecting critically

Purpose

Assessing creative thinking in schools hardly ever happens. Yet all teachers know that, in schools, what gets measured gets done. This activity explores some key principles for you to consider when introducing the idea of assessing creative thinking to staff. It suggests that evidencing progress in creative thinking requires the development of some different approaches to assessment.

Resources and setting up

- **Resource 24: Rethinking Assessment Figures**
- Access to Bill Lucas' report, *A Field Guide to Assessing Creative Thinking in Schools*[1]
- Access to the OECD's *Thinking Outside the Box*[2]
- Collections of various objects – A4 paper, stapler, sticky tape, magazines, sticky notes, large felt-tip pens, etc.
- **Resource 1: Five Creative Habits Framework** (for reference)

Getting going

STEP 1 15 minutes

The assessment of creativity goes back some 70 years, but while researchers have developed many well-used ways of measuring creativity, it's only in the last two decades – as national curricula have begun to specify habits/competences such as creative thinking – that educators have begun to consider the benefits of assessment. A decade ago, the Centre for Real-World Learning with Thomas Tallis School developed the five-dimensional model of creativity used in the playbook, and illustrated some ways in which the progress of young people's creativity could be tracked (see the first figure in **Resource 24**).

In 2022, the global testing body PISA introduced a new Creative Thinking test which has been used in more than 60 countries. In England, a new organisation, Rethinking Assessment, introduced the idea of a learner profile as a means of capturing a fuller range of pupils' strengths, including creative thinking (see the second figure in **Resource 24**).

Look at the two figures in **Resource 24**. What do you notice with regard to any other ways of assessing pupils you can think of? What do they suggest to you about how you might evidence the development of pupils' creative thinking in your school? Brainstorm some possible benefits and any challenges you can envisage.

---

[1] Lucas, *A Field Guide to Assessing Creative Thinking in Schools*.
[2] Organisation for Economic Co-operation and Development, *Thinking Outside the Box: The PISA 2022 Creative Thinking Assessment* (Paris: OECD Publishing, 2022). Available at: https://issuu.com/oecd.publishing/docs/thinking-outside-the-box.

Going deeper

STEP 2 25 minutes

Research suggests that there are two ways we can notice creativity in action: either by watching and listening in on a creative process or evaluating the creative products produced, such as prototypes, pictures, presentations, exhibitions and so on. For example, we might notice how creative an end product is by looking at a pupil's portfolio of work produced in response to a task. Alternatively, we might notice how creative the process of undertaking that task is by observing how a particular pupil (or group of pupils) exercises their imagination (or other creative habit) in responding to it.

To help colleagues understand the two ways in which pupils can demonstrate their creativity, plan a professional development activity in which staff are asked to undertake this task. Use the objects you've been given to create a new product.

Split each group into makers and observers. Give the makers 10 minutes to create a prototype product. Ask the observers to reflect on how they found the process of noticing creative thinking in their group of makers. Share your reflections.

What does this process suggest to you about what staff will need to be able to do in their classrooms?

STEP 3 15 minutes

Evidence from schools that have begun to assess the creative thinking skills of their pupils suggests five key learning points:

1. Make the invisible visible.
2. Create a culture of reflection.
3. Plan opportunities to demonstrate creativity.
4. Make assessment as authentic as possible.
5. Assess pupils over time.

With regard to the first point, for example, this might involve displaying a version of **Resource 1** in each classroom, developing icons for each of the creative habits, creating an area of the classroom walls where examples of work exemplifying each habit can be displayed, making a point of naming the creative habits demonstrated by pupils in their learning and so on.

In pairs, take each of the other four points and discuss ways in which you could respond to the suggestions.

The sixth learning point is to build teacher confidence in a broad range of assessment methods, which is the focus of the next activity.

Reflecting together

STEP 4 5 minutes

- What are the potential benefits of assessing creative thinking?
- What challenges do you anticipate, and how might you overcome them?

Your reflection notes

Activity 25
Develop Creativity Assessment Literacy Among Staff

1 hour 15 minutes

This activity might develop your creative habit of being ...

Playing with possibilities
Making connections
Using intuition

Purpose

To support the development of creative thinking, a special kind of assessment literacy is needed: the ability to understand the different assessment processes and their purposes, and to use them when evidencing creative thinking. This activity explores this kind of assessment literacy, introduces the idea of a creative thinking learning progression and suggests three robust assessment methods to use. It also invites you to consider which systems may need to be changed.

Resources and setting up

- Copies of **Resource 25: A Repertoire of Methods for Assessing Creative Thinking**
- Copies of **Resource 26: Learning Progression for 'Inquisitive'**
- Copies of **Resource 27: Pupil Self-Report for 'Inquisitive'**
- A range of examples of pupils' work in progress as well as final copies/presentations, etc.
- If available, Chapter 6 (Signs of Success) from Bill Lucas and Ellen Spencer's *Teaching Creative Thinking*[1]

Getting going

STEP 1 10 minutes

While assessing creative thinking may, at first glance, seem a very different activity for teachers from, say, assessing progress in maths or art and design, the core processes are similar. First, teachers need to understand what creative thinking is (the five habits) and then be able to learn how to notice progress over time as pupils gain in confidence and expertise. Finally, they need a repertoire of assessment methods that they're comfortable using.

The main leadership challenge here is to provide opportunities for teachers to explore approaches to assessment in a safe environment. This involves:

- Creating opportunities for the moderation of pupils' work/products.
- Encouraging teachers to see that assessing creative thinking is an opportunity for using assessment as a learning method to build a shared understanding of creativity.
- Giving teachers feedback to help them be more precise in their choice of pedagogies.

Ask colleagues what associations they have with the words 'assessment' and 'creativity' and capture these to reflect on later.

---

1 B. Lucas and E. Spencer, *Teaching Creative Thinking: Developing Learners Who Generate Ideas and Can Think Critically* (Carmarthen: Crown House Publishing, 2017), pp. 159–180.

---

80 | Play 7 **Track Progression in Creative Thinking**

STEP 2 10 minutes

Exploring. Start by considering **Resource 25**, ideally referring to Chapter 6 (Signs of Success) in *Teaching Creative Thinking*. Share examples of any of the methods listed that are already being used. In groups, choose one method and brainstorm how it might be used in a classroom to assess creative thinking.

STEP 3 30 minutes

Thinking in threes. A key principle when assessing complex skills is to get a number of viewpoints, sometimes referred to as 'triangulating'. In this way, you don't have to worry about any one 'measurement' being exactly right as it'll be considered in the light of the other two. To build confidence among staff, try these three methods:

- Teacher criterion-referenced grading (see **Resource 26**).
- Pupil self-report questionnaires (see **Resource 27**).
- Portfolios.

Check that all three methods are understood (use Chapter 6 from *Teaching Creative Thinking* to help you). Choose a specific class/subject known to you and a topic currently being taught. In groups, imagine what a pupil known to you might say on the inquisitive questionnaire. Using **Resource 26**, discuss the level of creative thinking you're seeing from the examples of pupils' work across its three sub-elements. Consider how you might organise portfolios (hard copy or digital, or both) to provide evidence for your moderation discussions.

Going deeper

STEP 4 15 minutes

Thinking about professional learning and systems. Leaders and teachers need the basic understanding and confidence to use the three methods in step 3. It's the leader's role to provide the systems to support the assessment of creative thinking. In groups, use these topic headings to start to consider which systems to explore:

- Using displays in classrooms to make creative thinking visible.
- Providing pupil-friendly descriptions of progress.
- Developing a bank of useful assessment materials.
- Creating opportunities for teachers to moderate pupils' work.
- Creating opportunities for teachers to observe each other.
- Including comments on creative thinking in school reports.

What else would you want to consider?

Reflecting together

STEP 5 10 minutes

- Have these activities changed your initial thinking about the relationships between creativity and assessment? If so, how?
- Which systems will you consider changing? How will you prioritise them?

Your reflection notes

Play 8
Ensure Professional Learning

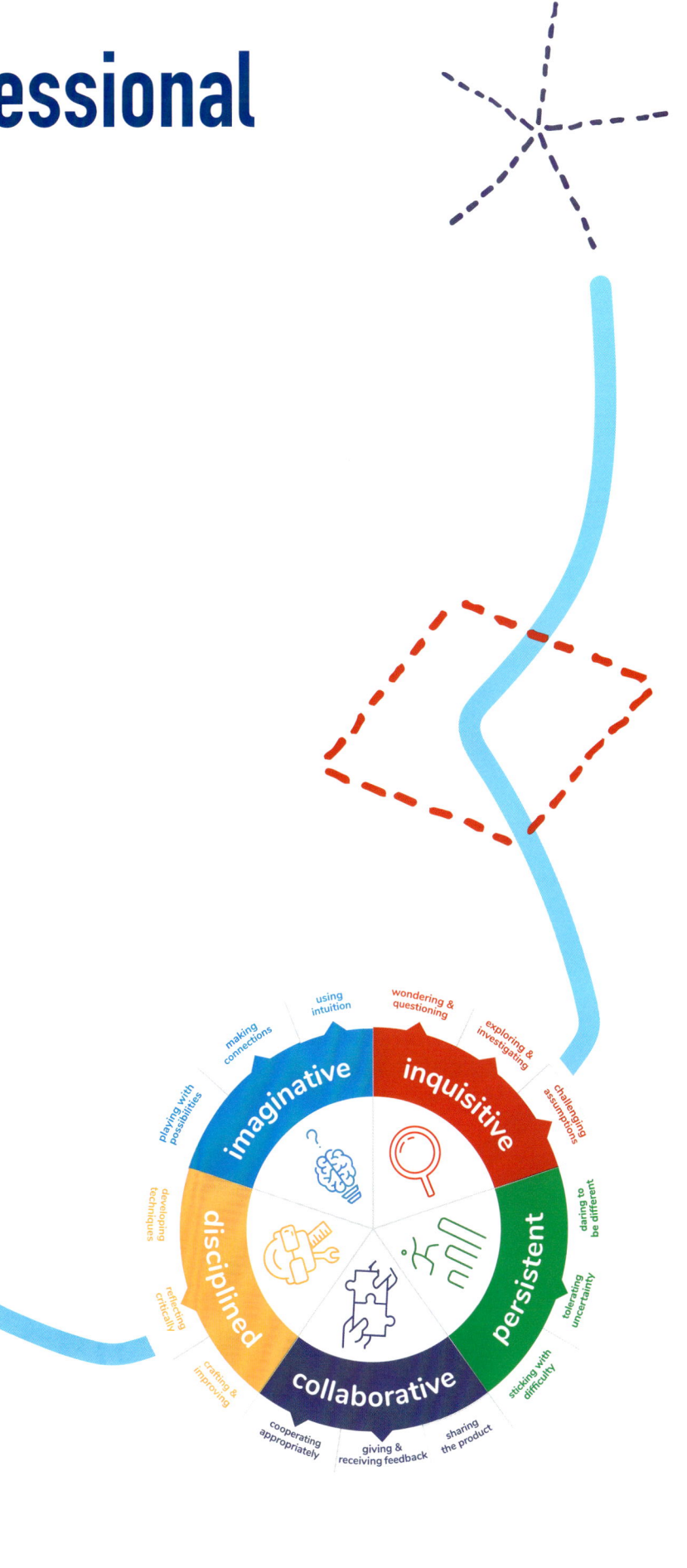

Activity 26
Create Opportunities for Powerful Professional Learning

🕐 1 hour to 1 hour 20 minutes

This activity might develop your creative habit of being ...

- inquisitive
- persistent
- collaborative
- disciplined — Reflecting critically
- imaginative — Making connections, Playing with possibilities

Purpose

Powerful professional learning enhances practice and makes a difference for pupils' learning. This activity encourages your team to reflect on what you've learned from prior experiences of professional learning and how these might be applied to or adapted to professional learning for creativity and creative thinking.

Resources and setting up

- Copy and cut up the cards contained in **Resource 28: Twenty Professional Learning Activity Cards**. Put them face down in a pile, reserving the blank card.
- Copy **Resource 29: Powerful Professional Learning Grid** onto four sheets of A3 paper or create your own grid on a large sheet of paper.

Getting going

STEP 1 20 minutes

This activity is designed for a team of three to six people, including anyone with overall responsibility for professional learning and, ideally, the person with oversight of teaching and learning.

Shuffle the cards from **Resource 28** and select the top one. Using the grid from **Resource 29**, write the name of the professional learning activity in the left-hand column, and then work along the row and consider each of the questions. When you get to the last two columns, use your imagination to think of ways to enhance the professional learning activity or strategy to develop teachers' creativity and creative thinking, and about how the activity can help teachers to develop pupils' creativity and creative thinking.

Which of these approaches is your school already using?

84 | Play 8 **Ensure Professional Learning**

Going deeper

STEP 2 20–40 minutes

As there are a number of activities and the process is repetitive, you may want to do this over two or three sessions fairly close together. Alternatively, you might split into two groups, each taking some of the cards and working through the process before sharing and verifying your responses with your colleagues.

When you've gone through all the cards, check if any professional learning processes are missing. Write these on the blank card and go through the entire process again, photocopying another grid sheet if needed.

When you've completed the grid, look through all of your responses and reflect together on the following questions. This activity would work well if you're part of a wider professional learning community or collaborative and want to capture good ideas from across your networks.

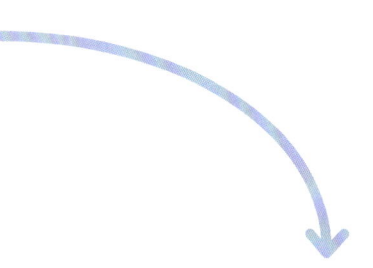

Reflecting together

STEP 3 20 minutes

- What strikes you about making professional learning powerful?
- What have you learned about resolving professional learning difficulties and challenges that you can draw on as you develop professional learning for creativity and creative thinking?
- What is similar and different about professional learning for creativity and creative thinking?
- What do you think the best activities will be?
- What will be your next steps?

Your reflection notes

Play 9
Collaborate with External Partners

Activity 27
Nurture and Learn with External Partners

⏱ 1 hour 10 minutes

This activity might develop your creative habit of being ...

- **Wondering & questioning** (inquisitive)
- **Sticking with difficulty / Daring to be different** (persistent)
- **Cooperating appropriately** (collaborative)
- **Making connections / Playing with possibilities** (imaginative)

Purpose

Creative collaboration with partners moves beyond short-term or off-the-shelf partnerships towards the consideration of mutually beneficial goals to maximise its return for all stakeholders. This activity helps you to consider potential partnerships within your community for the purpose of such collaboration. Although the activity is primarily for school leaders, governors/trustees and parents could also be invited for their rich source of local knowledge and connections.

Resources and setting up

- A set of **Resource 30: Peer Learning Prompt Cards** for each table
- An A3 piece of card/cardboard for each group
- A pack of materials for each group – contents might include modelling clay, Lego, straws, lollipop sticks, wool, paperclips, etc.
- Blank A5 cards
- A5 cards with a school development priority written on each one
- Two pieces of rope or two hula hoops placed on the floor, overlapping like a Venn diagram

Getting going

STEP 1 5 minutes

As an icebreaker, at tables in groups of five, read and respond to the prompt cards on your tables and share:

- Any experiences you have of working in partnership within the community.
- What benefits there might be for both the school and the community partner to work in partnership.

88 | Play 9 **Collaborate with External Partners**

STEP 2　15 minutes

Remaining at your tables, work together to create a map of the school community using the card/cardboard as a base and the materials provided. Try to make key landmarks identifiable (e.g. school, places of worship, supermarket).

After 10 minutes, invite the groups to walk around the room and look at each other's maps.

- Has everyone thought about the community in the same way? How are they the same? How are they different?
- Is the school community in the vicinity of the building, or is the school community of today much broader, including the virtual world?

Going deeper
STEP 4　30 minutes

The next challenge is to match the needs to the assets and consider:

- In what ways might the asset be able to support the need?
- In what ways might the need be an opportunity for the asset?

Organise yourselves into pairs (or groups) to share ideas and play with possibilities. Come together to discuss ideas. Nominate a scribe to write down the ideas and place them in the centre of the Venn diagram.

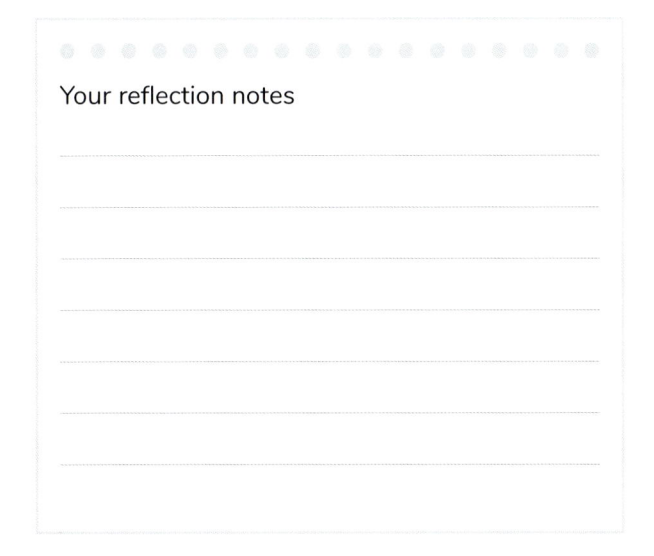

Your reflection notes

STEP 3　10 minutes

Return to your maps to identify assets within the community, writing the names on the A5 cards. These might be people, organisations or institutions with whom the school has already worked, or those they're aware of but haven't partnered with.

Everyone gathers around the Venn diagram on the floor and places the A5 cards with their assets in the circle on the right. As you're doing this, place the school development priority cards in the circle on the left. These are the school's 'needs'.

Reflecting together
STEP 5　10 minutes

- How might the ideas and partnerships suggested offer opportunities to ignite and develop creative thinking?
- What are your reflections on including parents and governors/trustees in this activity?
- This activity has highlighted the need for external partnership working to be relational rather than transactional; therefore, these relationships require an investment of time and attention to nurture them. Who might be able to support you with this?
- Where might there be funding or other resources available to support the ideas in the centre of the Venn diagram?
- What are your next steps?

Activity 27 **Nurture and Learn with External Partners**

Activity 28
Learn with Other Schools

🕐 5½ hours over a few weeks

This activity might develop your creative habit of being . . .

inquisitive
Wondering & questioning
Exploring & investigating
Challenging assumptions

persistent
Sticking with difficulty
Daring to be different
Tolerating uncertainty

collaborative
Cooperating appropriately
Sharing the product

disciplined
Developing techniques
Reflecting critically

imaginative
Playing with possibilities
Making connections
Using intuition

Purpose

Developing external networks across schools is important for mutual support and challenge around creative thinking. Peer learning visits and review can be valuable ingredients towards activating powerful networks, with opportunities to share and observe practice in leading for creativity. They also provide a forum for dialogue around teaching and learning, and a culture of openness for nurturing pupils, staff and your own creativity.

This activity uses an inquiry approach, taking you through a process of thinking about your learning goals, preparing for the visit, observing and investigating, reflecting, sharing and, finally, making connections with your existing knowledge and understanding. We encourage you to prepare for your visit by consciously opening yourself up to the learning experience and tapping into your creative habits.

Resources and setting up

- Other schools to work with. This activity is for leaders who already have an external network; if you don't, why not visit a site like https://www.creativityexchange.org.uk to learn from what other schools have been doing. It would be a good idea to work in a group of three or four schools, with the group visiting each of the schools during a peer learning cycle.

- **Resource 31: The Peer Learning Cycle**, which lays out the steps in infographic form.

Play 9 **Collaborate with External Partners**

Getting going

STEP 1 1 hour preparing for your visit

The host school:

There's no set agenda for the host school; you're in the driving seat and can decide what the visitors see and do, although the focus should be directed towards creative leadership (in practice).

As a priority, allow your visitors to observe some of your daily routines, whether speaking to staff during morning briefing or undertaking a learning walk. You may also choose to introduce visitors to a range of people including pupils, teachers, teaching assistants, parents or governors. You might decide to present a range of school policies, teaching and learning documents or external communications, such as newsletters.

As a host, draw on your persistence:

- How can you dare to be different?
- How can you tolerate uncertainty?

The visitors:

Conversations with your peer learning group are central to the learning visit cycle, before, during and after. In your first conversation, consider some of these questions before your visit:

- What are you hoping to learn from the school visit?
- Thinking about your theory of change (see **Activity 10: Use a Theory of Change**) and what you're hoping to achieve over the next phase in your timeline (see **Activity 11: Hang Out the Change Plan**), how might this school visit help you? Can you identify two areas?
- Being imaginative, how can you enter this experience ready to play with possibilities? What hidden cognitive or cultural biases might be holding you back?

STEP 2 3 hours

Peer learning visit:

Your host will have arranged the schedule for the visit and selected what they want to show you. However, we encourage you to generate your own list of questions based on the 10 categories of creative leadership (see **Activity 9: Creative Leadership in Action**), but as you do so, consider how your questions are framed as an invitation for learning and for developing trust and partnership. Here are some examples:

- What is the language and agreed definition of creativity in the school? How have you made it visible and ensured it's shared by everyone?
- What actions have leaders taken to identify change catalysts?
- How are leaders nurturing their own creativity and modelling it to others?

Consider how you'll capture the key information from the visit quickly – for example, through photographs (if given permission by the host school), drawings, words or mind maps.

STEP 3 1 hour

Peer group reflection and host school feedback: Following the visit, meet with your peer learning group once again. Take it in turns to consider some of these questions, but also add your own:

- What resonated with you and why?
- What were the creative leadership strengths of the school?
- How did these strengths happen – who did what and when?
- What sparked your inquisitiveness?
- To what extent did the visit meet your learning needs?

Finally, what can you feed back to the host school to enter into dialogue with them and help them to reflect on what is working, what is emerging and what else is possible? Be specific and descriptive.

Going deeper

STEP 4 15 minutes

Follow-up actions: Following the school visit and reflection, create an action plan. The school visit should lead to something different in your practice and/or setting; however, rather than grand changes, think about this as an iterative process of small tangible movements in your professional learning and understanding.

The host school:

- What did your visitors notice as your strengths? Did you agree/disagree?
- What ideas and/or observations did your visitors engage with?
- Did anything surprise you from the feedback you received?
- How will you integrate the visitors' feedback and your reflections into your practice? What are your next three steps?

The visitors:

- What new ideas can you trial? What are your next three steps?
- How can you apply the learning from your school visit to your own setting? Who do you need to speak to/what do you need to do?
- If you put new actions in place, what might be the outcome – what are you hoping to achieve?
- How will you share your experience with others?

Reflecting together

STEP 5 15 minutes

- How has this peer learning cycle supported your understanding of creative leadership?
- What has been valuable and/or challenging about this process?
- What might you do differently in the next peer learning cycle?
- How would you like this experience to impact your school?

Your reflection notes

Activity 29
Foster Creative Mindsets By Looking Outside Education

🕐 1 hour

This activity might develop your creative habit of being ...

Wondering & questioning
Exploring & investigating
Challenging assumptions

Daring to be different

Cooperating appropriately

Reflecting critically

Making connections

Purpose

This activity is for you to explore and better understand the benefits of learning with and from practitioners outside the education sector. Fostering a creative mindset can be challenging, but by connecting with creative practitioners who work within a different paradigm, you can learn from one another and begin to think like artists or engineers (or whoever you're partnering with).

Resources and setting up

- We suggest that this activity is facilitated in a different room from the one in which you work normally. Therefore, if previous activities have been in classrooms or conference rooms, perhaps this one could be conducted in the library, outside (if weather permits) or off-site in a local community space.
- Flip chart and pens for each group.
- Copy and print **Resource 32: Richards and Hadaway Reading** and place a copy on each table.
- Be imaginative and dare to be different by recreating the six quotes below in different formats and placing them around the space – for example, write one in chalk on the floor, write one on a sticky note hidden inside an object or place one in an envelope addressed to a participant.

   1. The creative practitioners that we worked with didn't seem to have the same pressures on them as teaching staff seem to have. They didn't seem hung up on skills and evidence but more focused on context, engagement, the story, developing creativity.

   2. Having your ideas and ways of teaching challenged by a creative practitioner who isn't a teacher is at the same time terrifying and refreshing.

   3. It's for this reason that I was able to observe something that challenged my understanding of successful teaching. Exposure to a contrasting style of delivery helped to reinforce the notion that success is defined by outcome rather than a predefined set of qualities.

   4. The process of being imaginative and 'forcing', initially, my thinking to be more 'outside the box', has been refreshing and invigorating.

5. I feel that I am more prepared to take risks without the worry of 'What happens if things go wrong?'
6. I loved breaking away from the timetabled curriculum and having the freedom to follow a more fluid, dynamic and developmental teaching style. I feel freer to explore. I still feel revitalised in my approach to teaching and delivery of the wider curriculum and now am more dynamic in my approach.[1]

Getting going

STEP 1 5 minutes

In groups, consider the question from **Resource 32** and share your initial thoughts with each other:

- What characteristics might a 'hybrid' creative practitioner teacher possess, and in what ways could these characteristics benefit a teacher's practice.

Each group writes down their best initial answer on flip chart paper.

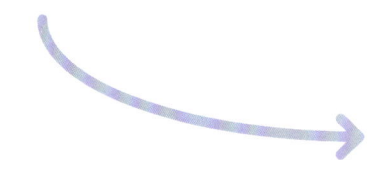

STEP 2 20 minutes

There are six quotes from the teachers involved in the Richards and Hadaway research paper available around the space, each relating to teachers' thoughts on working with creative practitioners. Some may be more visible than others, but everyone looks for them together. When someone finds the first quote, the searching stops.

The first quote is read out, and the participants reconsider and build on their initial responses to the starter question from **Resource 32**, starting with: 'Could it be that …?'

After a few minutes, the search for quotes continues until the next is found. Everyone moves on to the second quote and repeats the action, building on their responses each time and drawing on their inquisitive capabilities. Continue until the final quote is discovered.

STEP 3 10 minutes

The list below contains features from artist and engineer signature pedagogies.[2] Have a conversation about how these differ from the standard orthodoxy in classrooms.

The use of:

- Different learning environments.
- Provocation.
- Leaving room for the unexpected.
- Play.
- Classroom discourse for problem-solving.
- Collaborative working.

---

1   N. Richards and S. Hadaway, Inter-Professionalism Between Teachers and Creative Practitioners: Risk, Exploration and Professional Identity – Learning in Situ and the Impact on Practice. *Practice*, 2: (2020): 38–52 at 44, 48, 49, 50.
2   J. Hanson, S. Hardman, S. Luke, P. Maunders and B. Lucas, *Engineering the Future: Training Today's Teachers to Develop Tomorrow's Engineers* (London: Royal Academy of Engineering, 2018). See also P. Thompson, C. Hall, K. Jones and J. Sefton Green, *The Signature Pedagogies Project: Final Report* (Nottingham: University of Nottingham, 2012).

Going deeper

STEP 4 15 minutes

Share the film from Cambois Primary School: https://www.youtube.com/watch?v=uCiloghcYbs. This is a film from one of the schools in the North East Creativity Collaborative Network in England.[1] The staff worked alongside a creative practitioner over a series of twilight sessions to explore their understandings and misconceptions about creativity and how they could plan for developing their pupils' creativity.

Or share the film from Ysgol Aberconwy: https://vimeo.com/669832322. This is a project documentary for the Welsh programme Creative Learning Through the Arts.[2] The film focuses on one aspect of the programme's activities taking place in secondary schools which aims to embed creative learning practice, expertise and pedagogy.

Following the film, consider the following questions as a group:

- What could be the benefits of creative practitioners working alongside school staff during allocated professional learning time?
- How might the film support understandings of creativity in a different way?
- If you were to invite someone in to work with your staff, what would be the brief for the creative practitioner?

Reflecting together

STEP 4 10 minutes

- How has this activity solidified or changed your understanding of professional learning for creativity?
- You've looked at the impact of cross-sector working on teachers, but what could be the potential of you as leaders working alongside creative practitioners?
- Who in your network might be able to introduce you to suitable practitioners with whom you could begin to forge relationships?
- Identify an achievable goal you can work towards in the short term – for example, inviting a practitioner to work alongside you at an INSET.

Your reflection notes

---

1   Creativity Collaboratives is an Arts Council England funded programme to test a range of innovative practices in teaching for creativity: see https://www.creativityexchange.org.uk/creativity-collaboratives.
2   The Arts Council of Wales in partnership with the Welsh Government developed Creative Learning Through the Arts to put creativity at the core of Curriculum for Wales: see https://creativelearning.arts.wales/creative-learning/creative-learning.

Play 10
Reflect and Evaluate

Activity 30
Review and Fine-Tune

1 hour 20 minutes

This activity might develop your creative habit of being ...

inquisitive	persistent	collaborative	disciplined	imaginative
Exploring & investigating Challenging assumptions		Cooperating appropriately Sharing the product	Crafting & improving Reflecting critically	Using intuition

Purpose

This activity offers you an opportunity to pause and consider the progress your school is making towards creative thinking and how your creative leadership is impacting on any changes, as well as where you might need to focus your energies in the next phase. All teaching and teacher support staff should be involved in this review. You may also want to include pupil, governor/trustee, parent or school administration representatives.

Resources and setting up

This activity requires some preparation beforehand as you may find it helpful to have a range of data to draw on during the session.

- Flip chart paper with three columns titled 'Fruits', 'Shoots' and 'Roots'; one copy for each group
- One marker pen for each group
- Sticky notes

For leaders:

- Review your reflection notes from each activity, your journal entries and/or microblogs. Also review **Resource 9: Creative Leadership Plays – Notes**.
- What is your sense of the distance travelled, and how has your thinking developed?

For everyone:

- Revisit **Activity 3: Explore Creative Habits** and rework the creativity web activity, reflecting on how your understanding of creativity has evolved since you completed it the first time.
- Invite participants to bring with them any materials from previous activities or documents that have been updated following their ongoing professional learning in creative thinking.
- You'll also need a copy of your theory of change planning triangle from **Activity 10: Use a Theory of Change** to hand.

Getting going

STEP 1   10 minutes

To begin, have a conversation about your creativity web and what you've noticed about doing it the second time around. You might also share what you've noticed about yourselves and your confidence in leading for creativity.

STEP 2   5 minutes

In groups of five or six, participants work in silence during this step to add their responses to the flip chart as follows:

- Fruits – as a school, where have we succeeded in our transition towards creative thinking?
- Shoots – what is emerging but not yet fully developed?
- Roots – what has been seeded but not nurtured?

As there's only one marker pen, make sure everyone has an opportunity to hold the pen and write on the flip chart in the time available.

STEP 3   25 minutes

Now have a dialogue about the responses in each category, although you can also continue to add new responses if any come up.

Groups should select some responses and consider the following questions:

Fruits:

- What made that a fruit?
- What are its benefits?

Shoots:

- What does it need to become a fruit?
- What would be the best outcome for ___?

Roots:

- What does it need to break through the earth and develop a shoot?
- What can we do to make that happen?

You may want to draw on the materials and documents you've brought with you to support your points.

STEP 4   10 minutes

Finally, each group selects someone to feed back their most pertinent points to the whole group.

Activity 30 **Review and Fine-Tune** | 99

Going deeper

STEP 5 15 minutes

Share a copy of your final completed planning triangle from **Activity 10**. You have 15 minutes to talk about the following:

- What might need to be fine-tuned in light of the fruits, shoots and roots review?
- What has clearly been frostbitten, lost or requires rethinking?

Write your responses on sticky notes and stick them to your fruits, shoots and roots flip chart.

Reflecting together

STEP 6 15 minutes

- What surprised or challenged you about the progress you're making?
- Is the pace of your progress too fast, too slow or about right?
- What updates do you need to make to your theory of change?
- How has this activity helped you to evaluate the impact of your creative leadership?
- How can this playbook support you to reach your next goals – what might need to be revisited?

Your reflection notes

Call to action

This playbook and the creative thinking activities it contains illustrate some of what is possible in schools. It was designed to enable you to become braver, more intentional and more systematic in your own leadership practices.

We close the playbook by encouraging you to take action, linked to your values and the vision you have for your school. To support you in this, we've created an online professional learning space: leadingforcreativethinking.org.

With you, we want to build an education system that develops the creativity of teachers and pupils alike.

It's a high bar, something no education system in the world today yet does. But, together, as part of a passionate worldwide community of creative educators, we might just be able to make significant progress.

Come and join us!

RESOURCES

Resource 1
Five Creative Habits Framework

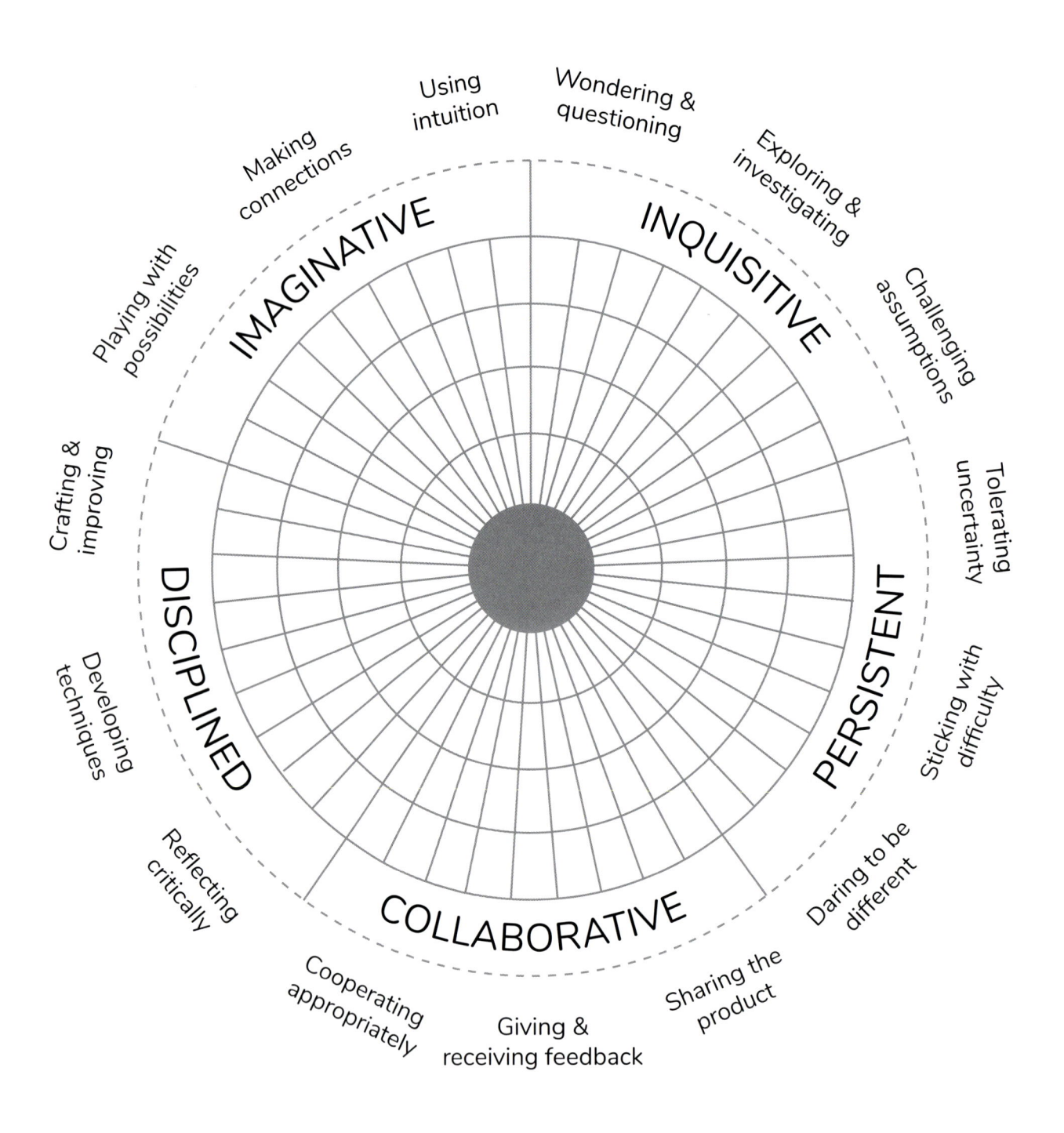

IMAGINATIVE
- Making connections
- Using intuition
- Playing with possibilities

INQUISITIVE
- Wondering & questioning
- Exploring & investigating
- Challenging assumptions

PERSISTENT
- Tolerating uncertainty
- Sticking with difficulty
- Daring to be different

COLLABORATIVE
- Sharing the product
- Giving & receiving feedback
- Cooperating appropriately

DISCIPLINED
- Reflecting critically
- Developing techniques
- Crafting & improving

Resource from *Creative Thinking in Schools* © Bill Lucas, Ellen Spencer, Louise Stoll, Di Fisher-Naylor, Nia Richards, Sian James and Katy Milne

Resource 2
Descriptions of the Creative Habits

Inquisitive	**Creative individuals are good at uncovering and pursuing interesting and worthwhile questions both in a specific subject and more generally.**
Wondering and questioning	Not simply curious, creative individuals pose concrete questions about things to help them understand and develop new ideas.
Exploring and investigating	Questioning things alone does not make a creative thinker. Creative individuals act out their curiosity through exploration and follow up on their questions by actively seeking and finding out more.
Challenging assumptions	It's important to maintain a degree of appropriate scepticism, not taking things at face value without critical examination.
Persistent	**Creative individuals don't give up easily.**
Tolerating uncertainty	Being able to tolerate uncertainty is important when actions or even goals aren't fully set out.
Sticking with difficulty	Persistence in the form of tenacity is important, enabling an individual to get beyond familiar ideas and come up with new ones.
Daring to be different	Creative thinking demands a certain level of self-confidence as a prerequisite for sensible risk-taking.
Collaborative	**Creative individuals recognise the social dimension of the creative process.**
Sharing the product	Creative outputs matter, whether they're ideas or things creating impact – functional or aesthetic – beyond their creator.
Giving and receiving feedback	Creative thinkers want to contribute to the ideas of others and hear how their own ideas might be improved.
Cooperating appropriately	Creative individuals cooperate with others, taking into account the nature of the group, the kind of problem and the stage that the group has reached. They seek out wisdom and guidance when it's needed and from the best available source.

Resource from *Creative Thinking in Schools* © Bill Lucas, Ellen Spencer, Louise Stoll, Di Fisher-Naylor, Nia Richards, Sian James and Katy Milne

Disciplined	**Creative thinking requires knowledge and skill to craft and shape the product or process.**
Reflecting critically	Evaluation is the way in which progress can be seen and understood and the quality of new ideas or novel thinking can be checked.
Developing techniques	Creative thinkers practise a range of conceptual and practical skills in order to improve.
Crafting and improving	Creative thinkers put learning into practice. Taking pride in their work, attending to details, practising, and correcting any errors are indicators of the highest levels of creative thinking.
Imaginative	**At the heart of creative thinking is the ability to come up with imaginative solutions and possibilities.**
Playing with possibilities	Developing an idea involves manipulating it, trying it out and improving it.
Making connections	Seeing new links between ideas is an important aspect of the synthesising process of creative thinking.
Using intuition	The use of intuition allows individuals to make new connections tacitly that would not necessarily materialise using analytical thinking alone.

Resource from *Creative Thinking in Schools* © Bill Lucas, Ellen Spencer, Louise Stoll, Di Fisher-Naylor, Nia Richards, Sian James and Katy Milne

Resource 3
Creativity Habits Web Template

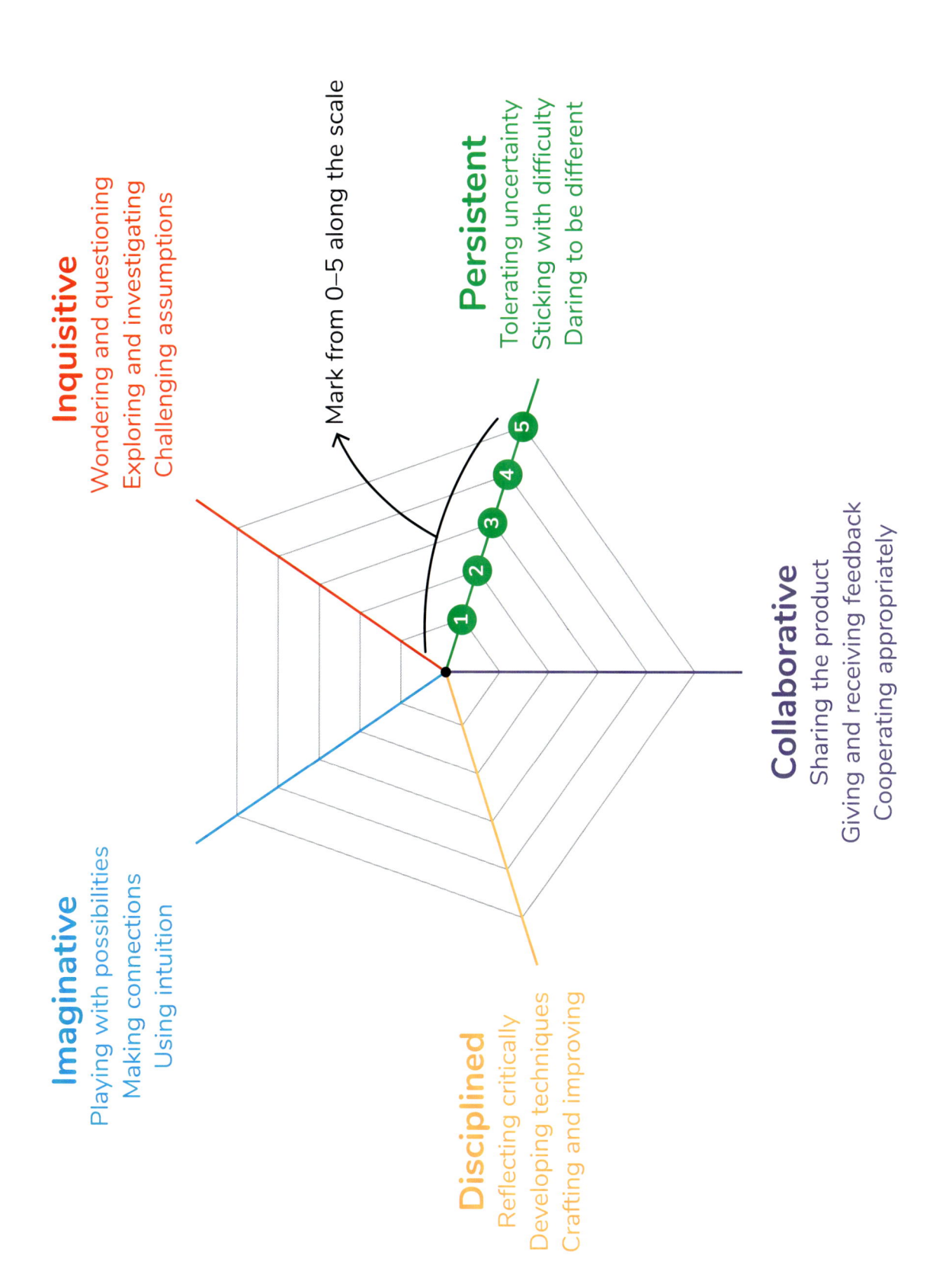

Inquisitive
Wondering and questioning
Exploring and investigating
Challenging assumptions

Persistent
Tolerating uncertainty
Sticking with difficulty
Daring to be different

Mark from 0–5 along the scale

Collaborative
Sharing the product
Giving and receiving feedback
Cooperating appropriately

Disciplined
Reflecting critically
Developing techniques
Crafting and improving

Imaginative
Playing with possibilities
Making connections
Using intuition

Resource from *Creative Thinking in Schools* © Bill Lucas, Ellen Spencer, Louise Stoll, Di Fisher-Naylor, Nia Richards, Sian James and Katy Milne

Resource 4
Creative Individuals Are …

Inquisitive	**Creative individuals are good at uncovering and pursuing interesting and worthwhile questions both in a specific subject and more generally.**
Wondering and questioning	Not simply curious, creative individuals pose concrete questions about things to help them understand and develop new ideas.
Exploring and investigating	Questioning things alone does not make a creative thinker. Creative individuals act out their curiosity through exploration and follow up on their questions by actively seeking and finding out more.
Challenging assumptions	It's important to maintain a degree of appropriate scepticism, not taking things at face value without critical examination.

Resource from *Creative Thinking in Schools* © Bill Lucas, Ellen Spencer, Louise Stoll, Di Fisher-Naylor, Nia Richards, Sian James and Katy Milne

Persistent	Creative individuals don't give up easily.
Tolerating uncertainty	Being able to tolerate uncertainty is important when actions or even goals aren't fully set out.
Sticking with difficulty	Persistence in the form of tenacity is important, enabling an individual to get beyond familiar ideas and come up with new ones.
Daring to be different	Creative thinking demands a certain level of self-confidence as a prerequisite for sensible risk-taking.

Resource from Creative Thinking in Schools © Bill Lucas, Ellen Spencer, Louise Stoll, Di Fisher-Naylor, Nia Richards, Sian James and Katy Milne

Collaborative	Creative individuals recognise the social dimension of the creative process.
Sharing the product	Creative outputs matter, whether they're ideas or things creating impact – functional or aesthetic – beyond their creator.
Giving and receiving feedback	Creative thinkers want to contribute to the ideas of others and hear how their own ideas might be improved.
Cooperating appropriately	Creative individuals cooperate with others, taking into account the nature of the group, the kind of problem and the stage that the group has reached. They seek out wisdom and guidance when it's needed and from the best available source.

Resource from *Creative Thinking in Schools* © Bill Lucas, Ellen Spencer, Louise Stoll, Di Fisher-Naylor, Nia Richards, Sian James and Katy Milne

Disciplined	Creative thinking requires knowledge and skill to craft and shape the product or process.
Reflecting critically	Evaluation is the way in which progress can be seen and understood and the quality of new ideas or novel thinking can be checked.
Developing techniques	Creative thinkers practise a range of conceptual and practical skills in order to improve.
Crafting and improving	Creative thinkers put learning into practice. Taking pride in their work, attending to details, practising, and correcting any errors are indicators of the highest levels of creative thinking.

Resource from *Creative Thinking in Schools* © Bill Lucas, Ellen Spencer, Louise Stoll, Di Fisher-Naylor, Nia Richards, Sian James and Katy Milne

Imaginative	**At the heart of creative thinking is the ability to come up with imaginative solutions and possibilities.**
Playing with possibilities	Developing an idea involves manipulating it, trying it out and improving it.
Making connections	Seeing new links between ideas is an important aspect of the synthesising process of creative thinking.
Using intuition	The use of intuition allows individuals to make new connections tacitly that would not necessarily materialise using analytical thinking alone.

Resource from *Creative Thinking in Schools* © Bill Lucas, Ellen Spencer, Louise Stoll, Di Fisher-Naylor, Nia Richards, Sian James and Katy Milne

Resource 5
Curriculum, Pedagogy and Assessment/Progression Venn

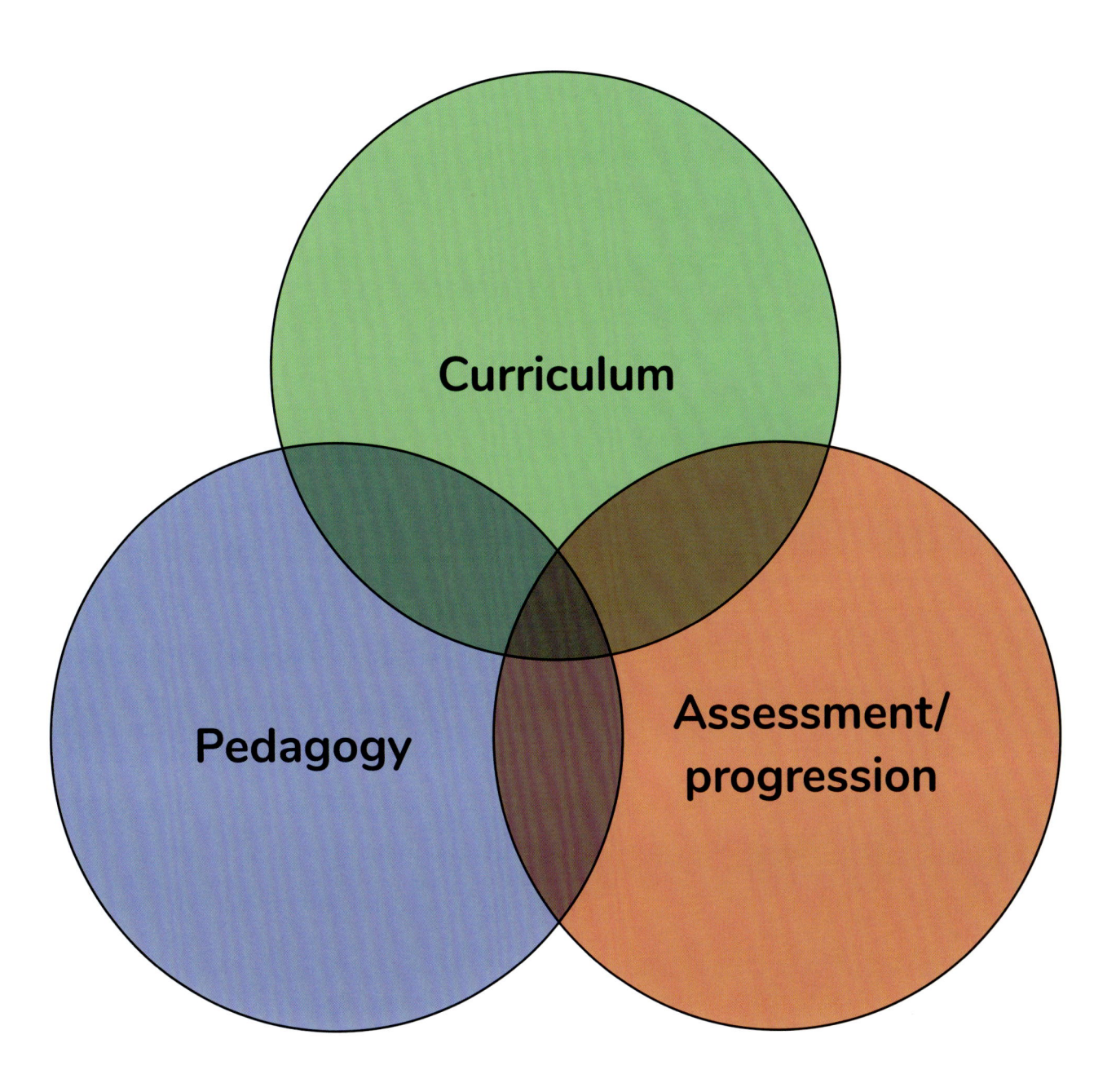

Curriculum

Pedagogy

Assessment/progression

Resource from *Creative Thinking in Schools* © Bill Lucas, Ellen Spencer, Louise Stoll, Di Fisher-Naylor, Nia Richards, Sian James and Katy Milne

Resource 6
Schools as Learning Organisations: Stimulating Environments for Creative Thinking

The focus of this playbook is the leadership needed to develop teaching for creativity and creative thinking in schools. But what kind of school offers the best home for such creativity to flourish? Our research suggests that SLOs provide such a setting. This is because SLOs are able to change and adapt routinely to new environments and circumstances as the people in them – individually, together and collectively – learn their way towards realising their vision.[1] A major change like embedding creativity right across a school requires such capacity.

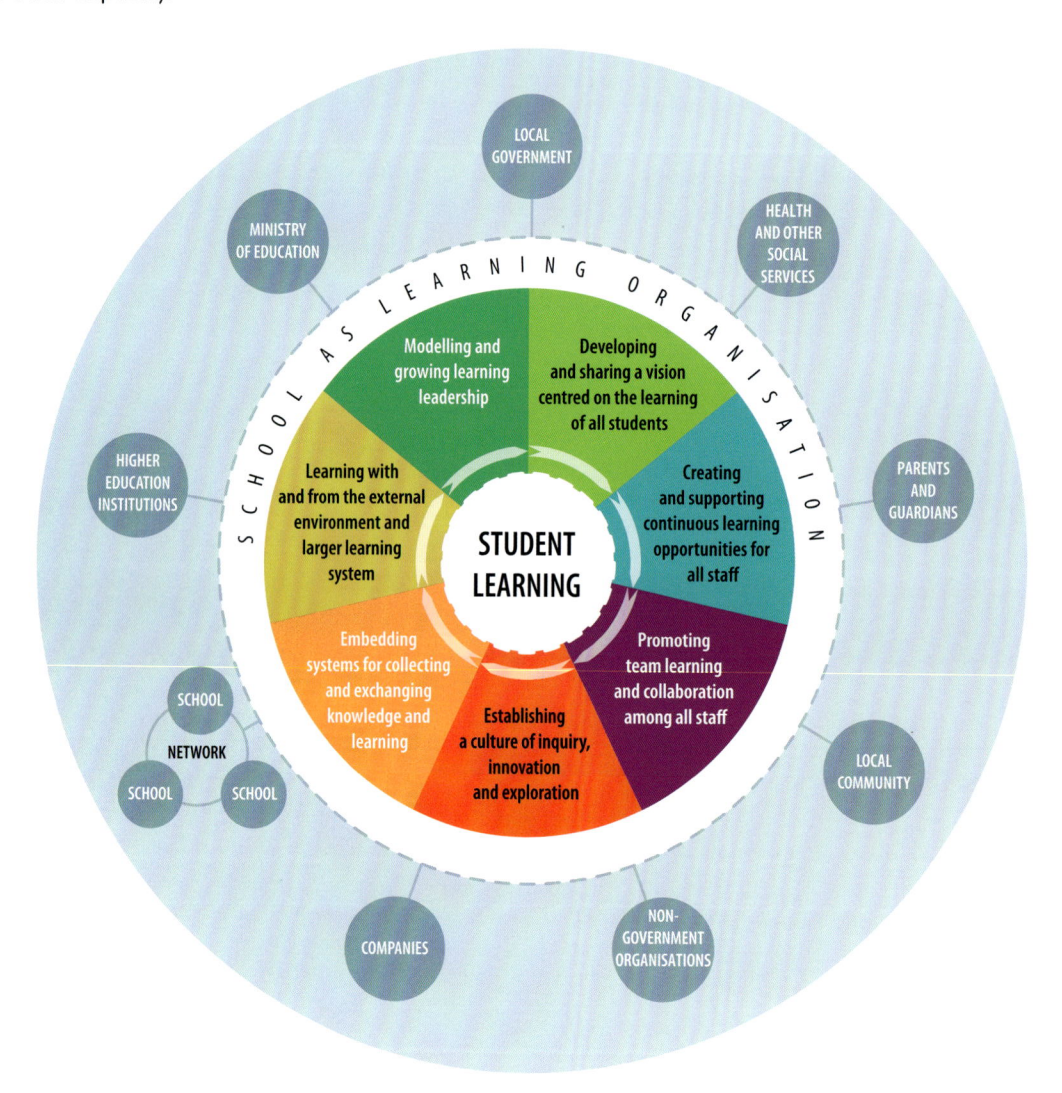

---

1 M. Kools and L. Stoll, *What Makes a School a Learning Organisation*? OECD Education Working Papers No. 137 (Paris: OECD Publishing, 2016). Available at: https://www.oecd.org/officialdocuments/publicdisplaydocumentpdf/?cote=EDU/WKP(2016)11&docLanguage=En; Organisation for Economic Co-operation and Development, *What Makes a School a Learning Organisation? A Guide for Policy Makers, School Leaders and Teachers* (Paris: OECD Publishing, 2016). Available at: https://www.oecd.org/education/school/school-learning-organisation.pdf.

Resource from *Creative Thinking in Schools* © Bill Lucas, Ellen Spencer, Louise Stoll, Di Fisher-Naylor, Nia Richards, Sian James and Katy Milne

The OECD's SLO model is a framework for schools and school systems to consider and bring to life in their own contexts as they work toward transforming their school(s) into environments in which significant innovations in curriculum, pedagogy and assessment can thrive.[2] For example, Wales has used the SLO model to support its schools in preparing for their new curriculum, and creativity features in the Welsh government's four purposes which are at the heart of the curriculum.[3]

In SLOs, collective endeavour concentrates on seven dimensions, as summarised below:

1. **Developing and sharing a vision centred on the learning of all pupils.** The SLO vision is focused on enhancing *all* pupils' learning experiences and outcomes. It may look as if nothing about this is particularly different from what any school might wish for – high quality and equity (for every pupil). Learning outcomes also include wellbeing – for example, satisfaction at school, motivation, sense of purpose, self-awareness and absence of anxiety. But SLOs go further: they think about both now and the future. They ensure that their vision and associated curriculum, pedagogies and assessment processes include capabilities that children and young people will need in their future, not their parents' past. And the vision–building process involves all staff, pupils, parents and other stakeholders to give them a shared sense of direction.

2. **Creating and supporting continuous learning opportunities for all staff.** The SLO consciously and consistently develops its staff. Everyone is involved in personally relevant, high-quality continuous professional learning. This starts with the end in mind, focusing on the problems staff face in their practice that specifically relate to pupil learning needs and the school's associated goals. Workplace and external learning opportunities blend together, and professional learning takes place over time, offering challenge and promoting reflection, analysis and practice. The school's culture and structures support this.

3. **Promoting team learning and collaboration among staff.** Colleagues learn how to think and act together, and they open up their practice to scrutiny. Staff observe each other and share their collective learning as they network and learn more about their learning together. Deep and meaningful cooperation between people is grounded in trust and mutual respect. Colleagues are given time to think together about solving problems, to have focused conversations, to extend their knowledge and to develop their practice.

4. **Establishing a culture of inquiry, innovation and exploration.** For a school to become a learning organisation, it's crucial that people dare to innovate in their practice. In such a school, the spirit of inquiry, initiative and willingness to experiment with new ideas and practices is pervasive. Staff are able and willing to avoid snap judgements, consider different perspectives, ask increasingly focused questions, and investigate and learn from problems in practice. All this leads to more informed decisions, greater confidence and adaptability.

5. **Embedding systems for collecting and exchanging knowledge and learning.** The school's processes, strategies and structures support staff in SLOs to learn and react quickly in uncertain and changing environments. Staff collect, analyse, exchange and regularly talk about relevant evidence, and revise their theories of how change will happen and their plans and strategies. SLOs are selective about the evidence they use, choosing it carefully to help them make wise decisions and move forward successfully in realising this vision.

6. **Learning with and from the external environment and larger learning system.** SLOs are highly attuned to global changes and deeply connected to what is going on in their local context. They know that they

---

2   The model is based on an extensive literature review and was adapted from Marsick and Watkins' (school as) learning organisation model, also taking account of related, more recent and cross-disciplinary literature and input from an expert network: V. Marsick and K. Watkins, Demonstrating the Value of an Organization's Learning Culture: The Dimensions of the Learning Organization Questionnaire. *Advances in Developing Human Resources*, 5(2) (2003): 132–151.
3   See https://hwb.gov.wales/professional-development/schools-as-learning-organisations; see also the OECD's review of progress: *Developing Schools as Learning Organisations in Wales: Implementing Education Policies* (Paris: OECD Publishing, 2018). Available at: https://www.oecd.org/education/Developing-Schools-as-Learning-Organisations-in-Wales-Highlights.pdf.

Resource from *Creative Thinking in Schools* © Bill Lucas, Ellen Spencer, Louise Stoll, Di Fisher-Naylor, Nia Richards, Sian James and Katy Milne

don't have all the answers to their challenges, so developing networks and powerful, respectful and equal relationships with many partners is essential to them. As a result, pupils benefit from extended offerings of rich and diverse learning experiences.

7. **Modelling and growing learning leadership.** Learning leadership binds the SLO together, providing direction for learning and ensuring that actions are consistent with vision, goals and values. School leaders are leaders of the curriculum and pedagogy that will help them to realise their vision, and they establish a learning culture and develop other learning leaders. They model and champion professional learning in and beyond their schools, and create a safe, trusting and creative culture and supportive structures. In being prepared for major change, leaders in SLOs often show considerable courage. Creative leadership is learning leadership specifically focused on the development of creativity and creative thinking.

Cross-cutting themes – the 4Ts (trust, time, technology and thinking together)[4] – also flow through the seven dimensions, with a fifth theme, compassion, also highlighted since the pandemic.[5] Together, the dimensions add up to a sustainable learning culture – a school that's ready for challenges that lie ahead.

---

4 Kools and Stoll, *What Makes a School a Learning Organisation?*, p. 32.
5 L. Stoll and C. Sinnema, Realising Curriculum Change Through Schools as Learning Organisations (SLOs) in Times of Crisis and Beyond. Paper presented at the International Congress for School Effectiveness and Improvement Virtual Congress, March 2021.

Resource from *Creative Thinking in Schools* © Bill Lucas, Ellen Spencer, Louise Stoll, Di Fisher-Naylor, Nia Richards, Sian James and Katy Milne

Resource 7
School as a Learning Organisation Plan

Using the dimensions to develop creative thinking[1]

Developing creative thinking across your school
- Developing and sharing a vision centred on the learning of all students
- Creating and supporting continuous learning opportunities for all staff
- Promoting team learning and collaboration among all staff
- Establishing a culture of inquiry, innovation and exploration
- Embedding systems for collecting and exchanging knowledge and learning
- Learning with and from the external environment and larger learning system
- Modelling and growing learning leadership

---

1   The figures on p. 117–118 draw on Organisation for Economic Co-operation and Development, *What Makes a School a Learning Organisation? A Guide for Policy Makers, School Leaders and Teachers* (Paris: OECD Publishing, 2016). Available at: https://www.oecd.org/education/school/school-learning-organisation.pdf.

Resource from *Creative Thinking in Schools* © Bill Lucas, Ellen Spencer, Louise Stoll, Di Fisher-Naylor, Nia Richards, Sian James and Katy Milne

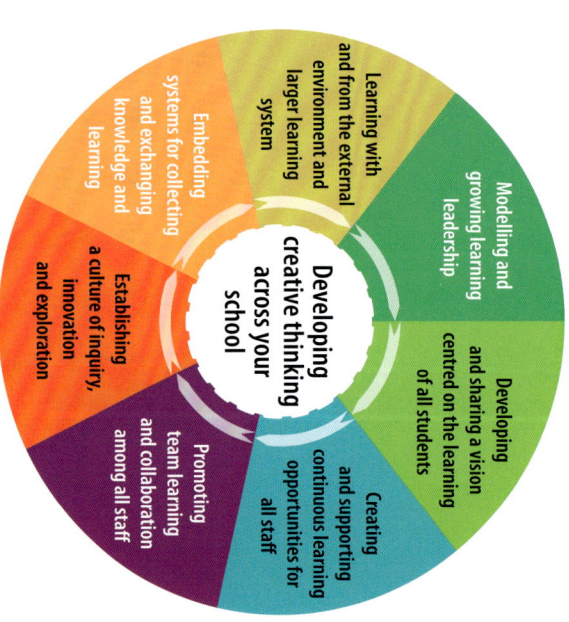

Using the dimensions to develop creative thinking

Learning with and from the external environment and larger learning system

---

Resource from *Creative Thinking in Schools* © Bill Lucas, Ellen Spencer, Louise Stoll, Di Fisher-Naylor, Nia Richards, Sian James and Katy Milne

Resource 8
Creative Leadership Plays

Creative Leadership Play 1: The Change Process

Articulate a clear description of the process of change, so everyone understands how young people's creativity will be developed.

Creative leadership involves change management. While the 10 plays you'll be talking about don't begin in completely unfamiliar territory, there's great potential for organisational change in each area the plays invite you to think about.

Part of this play of articulating a clear description of the process of change involves sharing your vision to ensure stakeholders are on board. Clear communication might involve things like writing creativity into the whole-school strategic plan, in whatever form that takes, or following up with whole-school professional development activities to ensure staff understand the value of creativity in their own subject. It might involve you including creativity in teaching and learning policies or regularly drawing attention to your half-termly 'habits' focus in your school newsletter to parents.

Creative Leadership Play 2: Develop Leaders

Identify and nurture creative change catalysts/teacher leaders.

While creative leaders are those senior leaders overseeing the whole of the school's plan for developing creativity in children through the 10 broad approaches we detail in this playbook, they don't act alone. Most obviously, there are the teachers in the classroom working with the tools of curriculum, pedagogy and assessment to teach for creativity. But, in order to see this happen school wide, there are essential functions served by many other individuals in a school. Any member of staff who takes an active role in developing teaching for creativity within the school, or a part of it, is a creative change catalyst. Your task, as a creative leader, is to identify, develop and enable those who would do this well.

It might be that there are individuals who have been given the task of developing creative thinking within their remit or subject area. They're likely to be a middle leader or teacher leader. Departmental heads, key stage leaders, teachers who lead specific school initiatives or pastoral leaders can all be well placed to perform the role of creative change catalyst, and may already have been asked to take this on.

There may be other individuals who believe wholeheartedly in the benefits of creativity but have not developed it beyond their own classroom or taken it into their middle leadership role. They may not have been identified, and your role as a creative leader is to spot them and enable them to make change in this area beyond the work they're already doing in their classroom or area of influence. This might be through structural changes, such as timetabling to release them to work with others, to network or to undertake training. It might be by giving them a formal role.

Teachers who fit this description can be given the role of creative champion, and tasked with developing creative thinking within their subject area or supporting colleagues to take risks and trial teaching for creativity approaches that develop creative thinking. Perhaps they will act as a coach or mentor, sharing knowledge and experiences and providing support and challenge. Or perhaps they will lead professional learning groups engaged in inquiry related to teaching for creativity to develop evidence-informed change. They might be involved in leading teacher learning within the school or across partnerships. As a creative leader, your role is to identify such individuals and provide them with the authority, support and resources they need to be effective.

Resource from *Creative Thinking in Schools* © Bill Lucas, Ellen Spencer, Louise Stoll, Di Fisher-Naylor, Nia Richards, Sian James and Katy Milne

As a creative leader, you can support creative change catalysts by setting professional development goals that are tied to their role via appraisal objectives. They also need support with time, resources and facilities to run creative projects and trial interventions in the classroom. In addition, they need to be developed professionally through investment in forms of learning that include wide reading.

Creative Leadership Play 3: Change the Culture

Create a culture in which creativity is promoted and valued in every aspect of the school's life and reflected in the school's improvement plan.

School culture is about the shared assumptions and beliefs that you, as a member of your school, have in common with other members. These taken-for-granted beliefs shape the way your school operates, the things you prioritise and the way your school interacts with the outside world. Culture can be 'seen' in the mindset of your teachers regarding the way they learn together, support one another and initiate change. If senior leaders develop a shared vision for the school that includes developing creative thinking in pupils, this will filter into the school's culture. It can also be 'seen' in ways the school's structures, systems and environment are organised – for example, reward systems, feedback mechanisms, timetabling decisions and marketing materials. As a creative leader, your role is to ensure that the vision for creativity filters into all aspects of culture.

In considering culture, your role might include working to ensure consistent messaging across the school, acting to empower staff to make creative decisions, ensuring creativity is kept in focus, promoting a learning mindset, making it 'safe' to be creative, valuing outcomes that go beyond the academic and modelling creativity to those you influence.

A vital task for you as a creative leader is to ensure consistent language when talking about creativity and creative thinking. Within the school's culture, there needs to be a consistent language for discussions about creativity and creative thinking. Leaders need to develop a common language for creativity so that everyone understands what it means.

To develop creativity in others, all staff need to be familiar with what being creative means and how to think creatively. Every leader needs to recognise what creativity is when they see it and know what they can do to develop it. And that's what your teachers need to be able to do as well.

Creativity language will be reinforced through constant use – for example, through the naming of key characteristics and behaviours of creative thinkers, through communication, through a clear framework for teaching and through the use of visual displays, newsletters and reading material in the library and for professional learning.

Language can be seen in job titles – for example, you might choose to have a director of creativity sitting within your leadership team. Language can also be seen in curriculum decisions – for example, you might choose to have a half-termly focus on a particular habit of mind.

Pedagogically, professional learning for your staff could aim to shed light on the different ways that 'imagination' might be seen in science, maths, art or design technology. It might explore different words used to describe what is happening when people are being creative. This is where a common framework of language can be helpful in your school.

Creative Leadership Play 4: Rethink Structures

Build creative thinking into all resourcing.

Channelling resources within your school is necessary for developing creativity. A consideration for creative leaders is how to ensure resources are allocated effectively into creative activities and projects. An opportunity cost is involved in that certain goals may need to be put to one side in order to focus on creativity. While planning is important, you may also want to have some element of spontaneity in the use

---

Resource from *Creative Thinking in Schools* © Bill Lucas, Ellen Spencer, Louise Stoll, Di Fisher-Naylor, Nia Richards, Sian James and Katy Milne

of your school's resources – for example, teachers should be able to act on opportunities for children to take part in creative or cultural opportunities as they arise. An example of targeted financial investment into resources for teacher development might be investing in library material for teachers that supports their research and development.

A valuable resource in schools is time. Developing creativity across the school requires careful planning which, of course, needs time. Leaders need to factor this in to enable staff to plan together. They also need to be creative about how they free up time for this planning to occur.

Creative Leadership Play 5: Develop a Creative Curriculum

Embed creativity into a coherent curriculum.

Various approaches exist to develop a broad curriculum that enables creativity. Incorporating interdisciplinary teaching and learning can offer the opportunity for your learners to consider breadth of knowledge, as well as how concepts learned in one area might apply to another or to a third area – for example, engineering, where science, maths and technology cross-populate.

The arts should be valued too because, while teaching creatively and teaching *for* creativity aren't the same thing, creative arts subjects can provide a gateway to more creative approaches to teaching – ones that develop pupils' faculties in critical evaluation, exploration and discovery. Investment in arts subjects may contribute to strong creative teaching and practice in your school.

An area of activity for creativity leaders is in ensuring that creativity is established at the planning level across all subject areas. To do this, teachers need to be developed to plan creatively so that creativity sits at the core of every subject. This can be done by asking your departments to include explicit opportunities for creativity in schemes of work.

As a creative leader, you can also embed creativity by bringing it in through extra-curricular means. This might involve off-timetable development days that focus on particular habits of mind, extended learning experiences or learning programmes that sit alongside the timetabled subjects. It could also involve assemblies, visiting speakers or tutor group activities. Creativity can be taught less directly through pupil participation in performances and clubs.

Creative Leadership Play 6: Rethink Pedagogy

Develop staff confidence in using teaching and learning methods that cultivate creativity.

An area of activity for creative leaders is in influencing teaching and learning through providing professional development for teachers that focuses on pedagogy and shows how creative practice is good practice. Development opportunities should encourage reflection on the ways that different subjects require creative thinking.

Pedagogical tools can help teachers with the concept of split screen teaching, an idea introduced in **Activity 8** and again in **Activity 21**. It has a dual focus on developing both content understanding and a specific learning disposition. Any lesson can be taught in a way that either helps or hinders creative thinking; split screen teaching aims to facilitate this.

As a creative leader, your focus on pedagogy might involve you supporting teachers to think about pedagogic strategies tailored to their particular subject, which might help to develop the different habits involved in creative thinking.

Creative Leadership Play 7: Track Progression in Creative Thinking

Find ways to assess that explicitly recognise progress in the development of young people's creativity.

If you're going to develop creativity, you need teachers and children to have a common understanding and to recognise what it looks like in a given subject. You need to plan for the development of creativity in schemes of work, and then to notice when it's being developed. In school, this will mean assessment of pupils but also of teachers. For your teachers, this might be linked to appraisal objectives, particularly where there's a named individual with responsibility for developing creativity in each subject area. For your children, development of creativity should make an appearance in reporting.

A role for creative leaders is to put in place good practice to support the tracking of pupil capabilities and skills across the different disciplines. This might take the form of a creative learning passport that complements traditional knowledge-based assessments and practice. It might involve learner feedback or journaling, or other ways of recognising development through award and recognition systems.

Creative Leadership Play 8: Ensure Professional Learning

Make creativity a focus of staff professional learning.

Teachers need access to high-quality opportunities for development in two main ways if they're to teach for creativity. The first is discrete professional learning sessions or awareness-raising events with a specific focus on creativity – for example, regular 'creative activity of the week' sessions in staff meetings, a creativity blog or professional development days where teachers can work through what creativity looks like in their own subject area. Creativity isn't restricted to art or 'making' but is about rigorous critical thinking, imagination, hard work and frequent failure. You'll want to help teachers to incorporate creativity into their own schemes of work.

The second way of helping your teachers to access development is through everyday learning experiences, such as working with colleagues in professional learning communities (PLCs). For example, PLCs might support peer observation, lesson study or practice-based research where teachers evaluate changes to their practice. They might involve creative champions working in partnership across curriculum teams. As a creative leader, you can create processes and structures that enable teachers to work collaboratively to improve classroom practice.

Creative Leadership Play 9: Collaborate with External Partners

Invest in external partners and funding to help develop creativity.

A key consideration for leaders building creativity is how to link with the wider learning ecosystem, including other schools; cultural, charitable and arts organisations; local businesses; industry partners; and science and research organisations. An area for creative leadership activity is in developing partnerships strategically to meet the needs of those partners as well as your school. 'Bridging' to external partners can reinforce your school's internal priorities. Good partnerships can set in motion a virtuous cycle if your involvement with other organisations signposts you to further opportunities, such as real-life projects, work experience and mentoring.

Creative leadership in curriculum planning might also involve a broader set of stakeholders than a leader's own immediate team. For example, leaders can work with those in the creative industries, local community organisations or higher education partners. Closer to home, creative leaders can also facilitate curriculum teams across schools working in partnership with one another, each team having a creative champion to consider teaching and learning (see **Play 2: Develop Leaders**).

Resource from *Creative Thinking in Schools* © Bill Lucas, Ellen Spencer, Louise Stoll, Di Fisher-Naylor, Nia Richards, Sian James and Katy Milne

Creative Leadership Play 10: Reflect and Evaluate

Explore, reflect on and evaluate your school's journey to creativity.

Creative leaders at all levels need to build reflection into the creativity journey. This means reflecting on current practice through audits that note where creativity is currently seen in your school and where it might spread. Reflection can include reviews of leaders' contributions to the school's promotion of creativity through creative leadership plays for which you have responsibility, take part in or help to champion.

Evaluation is critical for ensuring that creativity remains a priority over time. When things are going well, your reflection should also lead to celebration.

Resource from *Creative Thinking in Schools* © Bill Lucas, Ellen Spencer, Louise Stoll, Di Fisher-Naylor, Nia Richards, Sian James and Katy Milne

Resource 9
Creative Leadership Plays – Notes

Creative leadership play	What is this?	How does it help our school develop the creative thinking of our pupils?	Are we doing it? If so, how?
1. The Change Process: Articulate a clear description of the process of change, so everyone understands how young people's creativity will be developed.			
2. Develop Leaders: Identify and nurture creative change catalysts/teacher leaders.			
3. Change the Culture: Create a culture in which creativity is promoted and valued in every aspect of the school's life and reflected in the school's improvement plan.			
4. Rethink Structures: Build creative thinking into all resourcing.			
5. Develop a Creative Curriculum: Embed creativity into a coherent curriculum.			

Resource from *Creative Thinking in Schools* © Bill Lucas, Ellen Spencer, Louise Stoll, Di Fisher-Naylor, Nia Richards, Sian James and Katy Milne

Creative leadership play	What is this?	How does it help our school develop the creative thinking of our pupils?	Are we doing it? If so, how?
6. Rethink Pedagogy: Develop staff confidence in using teaching and learning methods that cultivate creativity.			
7. Track Progression in Creative Thinking: Find ways to assess that explicitly recognise progress in the development of young people's creativity.			
8. Ensure Professional Learning: Make creativity a focus of staff professional learning.			
9. Collaborate with External Partners: Invest in external partners, including other schools, to help develop creativity.			
10. Reflect and Evaluate: Explore, reflect on and evaluate your school's journey to creativity.			

Resource from *Creative Thinking in Schools* © Bill Lucas, Ellen Spencer, Louise Stoll, Di Fisher-Naylor, Nia Richards, Sian James and Katy Milne

Resource 10
Using a Theory of Change in Schools

Changing teachers' habits is hard; leaders need to think through the process of change in some detail. A useful way of speculating on any change you might want to make in school is the idea of a theory of change. Patricia Rogers wrote: 'A "theory of change" explains how activities are understood to produce a series of results that contribute to achieving the final intended impacts. It can be developed for any level of intervention – an event, a project, a programme, a policy, a strategy or an organization.'[1]

There are many different ways of visualising a theory of change, and the same words can be described in a number of ways by different authors, but at its simplest it's helpful to think about the three levels shown in the planning triangle on the following page: interventions, intermediate outcomes and final goals.[2]

The theory of change, in essence, invites us to work back from what we want to see altered (the impact, or final goal at the top of the triangle). We would consider the intermediate outcomes (shown in the middle level) that need to happen to bring about the desired impact, and then the interventions (or activities or inputs, shown at the bottom level) that will bring about those outcomes.

For example, we might propose that to cultivate learners' creativity, certain outcomes must be developed including things like a common language for creativity, capability in using appropriate pedagogies, capability in planning units of work to include a focus on both knowledge content and creative habits, and confidence to track pupils' progress in creativity. To arrive at these outcomes, a theory of change could suggest interventions such as use of a theoretical framework to explain what it means to be creative, consideration of the sorts of signature pedagogies teachers will use, or training for staff.

The essence of the theory of change process is the invitation it brings with it for users to work back from their goal to picture in detail the steps along the way to achieving it – a kind of reverse engineering. The planning triangle pictures the two steps that lead to the final goals by breaking the bigger goals down into a small number of intermediate goals and clearly describing the interventions considered to be likely to lead to these.

In addition to thinking about interventions, intermediate outcomes and final goals, the process offers opportunities to ask questions such as:

- What assumptions am I bringing to my planning?
- What would enable the changes I want to see?
- What resources will colleagues need?

---

1   P. Rogers, *Theory of Change, Methodological Briefs: Impact Evaluation 2* (Florence, UNICEF Office of Research, 2014), p. 1. Available at: https://www.unicef-irc.org/publications/pdf/brief_2_theoryofchange_eng.pdf.
2   B. Lucas, *Creative School Leadership* (Perth: FORM, 2021).

Resource from *Creative Thinking in Schools* © Bill Lucas, Ellen Spencer, Louise Stoll, Di Fisher-Naylor, Nia Richards, Sian James and Katy Milne

A planning triangle

Final goals

Intermediate outcomes

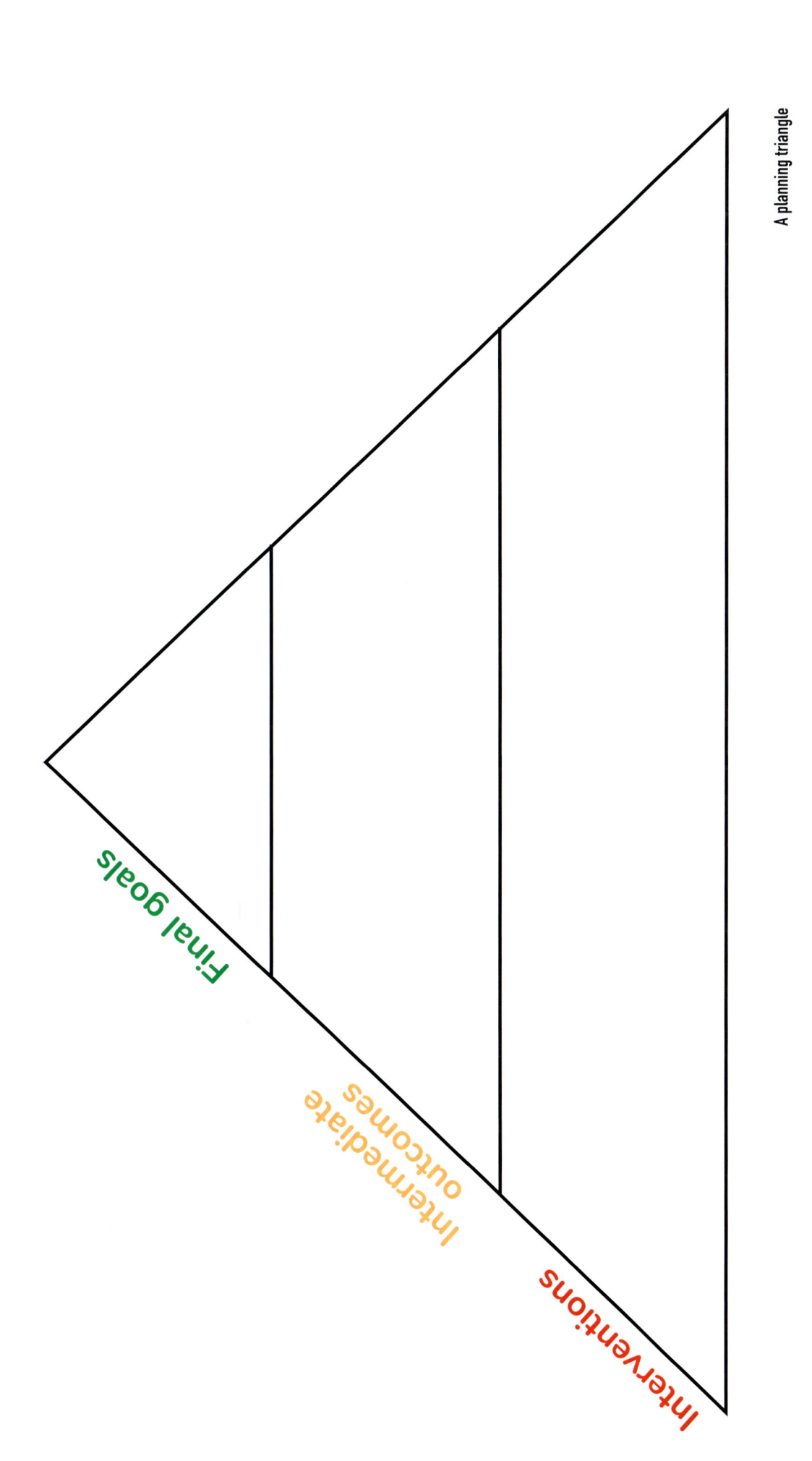

Interventions

Resource from *Creative Thinking in Schools* © Bill Lucas, Ellen Spencer, Louise Stoll, Di Fisher-Naylor, Nia Richards, Sian James and Katy Milne

Resource 10 **Using a Theory of Change in Schools** | 127

Resource 11
Intervention Cards

- Using the five habits
- Professional learning
- Active support from senior leaders
- Split screen curriculum planning

Resource from *Creative Thinking in Schools* © Bill Lucas, Ellen Spencer, Louise Stoll, Di Fisher-Naylor, Nia Richards, Sian James and Katy Milne

Staff time for curriculum planning	Using signature pedagogies
Project-based learning	Interdisciplinary learning

Trialling assessment methods	Using creative practitioners
Creative thinking lead teachers	Whole-school off-timetable days

Rethinking school reports

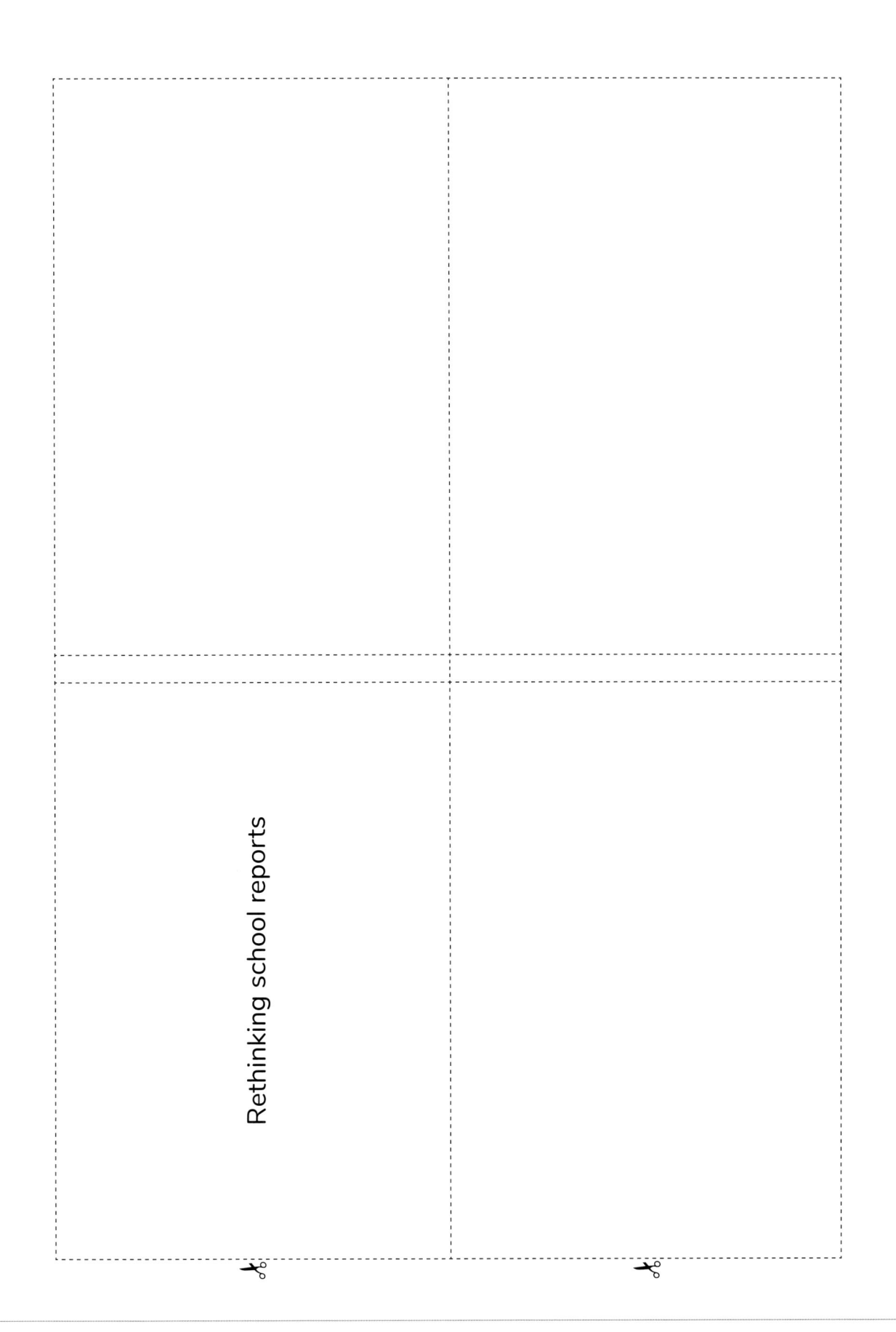

Resource from *Creative Thinking in Schools* © Bill Lucas, Ellen Spencer, Louise Stoll, Di Fisher-Naylor, Nia Richards, Sian James and Katy Milne

Resource 12
Thinking About How Social Networks Can Support Educational Change

Explanations for why major change initiatives and much smaller curricular or pedagogical innovations succeed or fail rest partly on what goes on between people in their social relations and the dynamics of these interactions. Change efforts flow through these relational links between educators, but people often don't pay sufficient attention to them. Informal webs of relationships often determine chiefly how well and how quickly change efforts take hold, diffuse and sustain. Relationships and support between colleagues are also central for the retention, increased professionalism and depth of engagement.

A network can be seen as 'a group of actors who are connected to one another through a set of different relations or ties'.[1] Researchers use social network theory (SNT) to help understand webs of relationships better. SNT focuses on the network of actors (people) in or across schools and school groups engaged with one another in various ways and degrees (e.g. through friendship, trust, seeking or giving advice or information). SNT can also help you to think about the complex relationship between formal structures in schools (e.g. use of time, planning, staffing) and informal patterns of interaction within and across organisations.

Too often, people assume that knowledge transfer moves rationally and predictably through formal continuous professional development experiences or some kind of professional learning community. But, when you look through the lens of a network, the types of knowledge and information any individual receives can be seen to depend upon social structure, position in the structure and the quality of ties in a network: 'who you know defines what you know'.[2]

Network maps – visualisations of complex patterns of interactions – highlight how the quantity and quality of relationships connect actors. Each actor is represented by a shape (a node). When these nodes are connected, arrows sometimes show who is seeking or providing resources (e.g. advice, information, social support), where ties are reciprocal (flowing in both directions), who has many connections, and who is isolated and so can't benefit from or access resources.

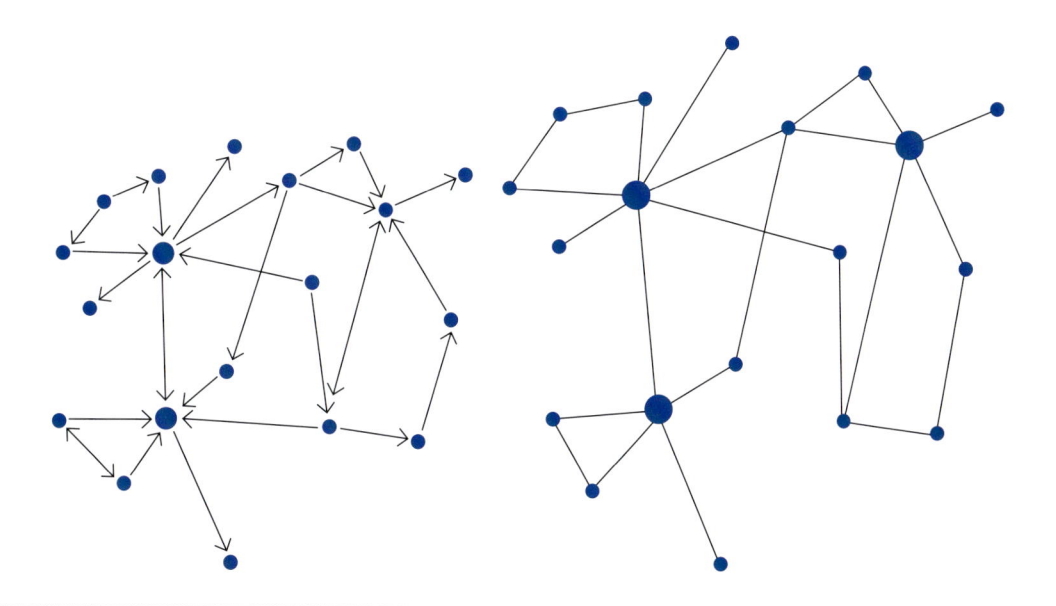

---

1 A. J. Daly, *Social Network Theory and Educational Change* (Cambridge, MA: Harvard Education Press, 2010), p. 4.
2 R. Cross, S. P. Borgatti and A. Parker, Making Invisible Work Visible: Using Social Network Analysis to Support Strategic Collaboration, *California Management Review*, 44(2) (2002): 25–46.

Resource from *Creative Thinking in Schools* © Bill Lucas, Ellen Spencer, Louise Stoll, Di Fisher-Naylor, Nia Richards, Sian James and Katy Milne

When members are closely connected to one another, networks are more cohesive. Resources flow easily through well-connected networks, and the network is more likely to stay together if and when the membership changes. Strong ties can develop between people who know each other well, and are particularly helpful in surfacing and sharing the tacit knowledge people have about their practice but don't talk about because of high levels of trust and emotional support. Weak ties are also important between people who know each other less well; if you only spend time with people you know very well, you often have similar knowledge. Weak ties give you access to a wider pool of diverse knowledge when it comes to creating new knowledge to solve complex educational problems.

Levels of activity can be measured through a network's density. Where more ties exist, a network is denser, and denser networks are more cohesive. Network size can influence this; it's easier to have everyone connected when there are fewer people. It's also important to know whether activity within a network is widely spread or mainly centralised around one or a smaller group of individuals. Where one or a few people hold all the power, it's completely centralised, and high levels of centralisation indicate a less cohesive network because removing a central figure would lead to a reduction of network activity.

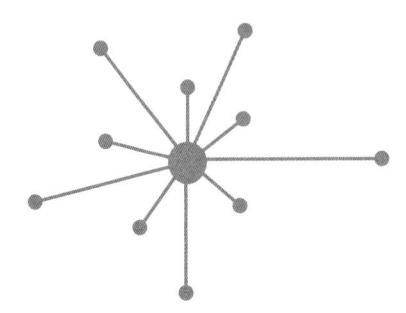

Much of this goes completely unnoticed in daily work life. As Lynda Gratton, professor of management practice at the London Business School, explains, 'What is happening here is almost below the surface. Most of us don't systematically track our networks and few companies have empirical data on how knowledge flows within and across their business.'[3] Lacking understanding of your networks is a missed opportunity.

---

3   L. Gratton, *Redesigning Work: How to Transform Your Organization & Make Hybrid Work for Everyone* (London: Penguin Random House, 2022), p. 28.

Resource from *Creative Thinking in Schools* © Bill Lucas, Ellen Spencer, Louise Stoll, Di Fisher-Naylor, Nia Richards, Sian James and Katy Milne

Resource 13
Common Change Challenges

- Perceived conflict with the accepted purpose of education
- Quality of teacher/leader training
- Accountability measures
- Narrow curricula and short-term measures
- Challenge of change and risk
- Resources (including time)
- Teachers' confidence with teaching for creativity
- Your own (and other teachers') creative habits of mind

Resource from *Creative Thinking in Schools* © Bill Lucas, Ellen Spencer, Louise Stoll, Di Fisher-Naylor, Nia Richards, Sian James and Katy Milne

Resource 14
Example Risk Matrix

Risk scores under 3 = very low risk, 3–4 = low risk, 5–9 = medium risk, 15–16 = high risk and 20–25 = extreme risk.

			Impact				
			Negligible	Minor	Moderate	Significant	Severe
		Rating	1	2	3	4	5
Likelihood	Very likely	5	5 Medium risk	10 High risk	15 Very high risk	20 Extreme risk	25 Extreme risk
	Likely	4	4 Low risk	8 Medium risk	12 High risk	16 Very high risk	20 Extreme risk
	Possible	3	3 Low risk	6 Medium risk	9 Medium risk	12 High risk	15 Very high risk
	Unlikely	2	2 Very low risk	4 Low risk	6 Medium risk	8 Medium risk	10 High risk
	Very unlikely	1	1 Very low risk	2 Very low risk	3 Low risk	4 Low risk	5 Medium risk

Resource from *Creative Thinking in Schools* © Bill Lucas, Ellen Spencer, Louise Stoll, Di Fisher-Naylor, Nia Richards, Sian James and Katy Milne

Blank risk matrix

		Impact				
		Negligible	Minor	Moderate	Significant	Severe
	Rating	1	2	3	4	5
Likelihood	Very likely — 5					
	Likely — 4					
	Possible — 3					
	Unlikely — 2					
	Very unlikely — 1					

Resource from *Creative Thinking in Schools* © Bill Lucas, Ellen Spencer, Louise Stoll, Di Fisher-Naylor, Nia Richards, Sian James and Katy Milne

Resource 15
Great Teacher Leader Characteristics

Great teacher leaders:

- **Are catalysts for change.** Great teacher leaders have drive and energy, understand how to lead change and confidently take the initiative. As change agents, they role model, develop motivational conditions to involve others and keep morale going in tough times. They're champions of improvement and distribute leadership to create other champions.

- **Have vision, purpose and goals.** Great teacher leaders are driven by strong moral purpose to ensure the best for all pupils. They lead learning and teaching with a clear vision, underpinned by strong core values and subject and pedagogical knowledge. With a strategic sense of the bigger picture, they think and plan ahead, while being adaptable as the need arises.

- **Communicate clearly.** Great teacher leaders share ideas, knowledge and plans clearly and transparently through regular face-to-face meetings and virtual learning environments. Meaningful, informal professional conversations are valued as important ways to connect and support development. They're outward facing, actively engaging with and visiting colleagues elsewhere.

- **Use research and school-based evidence.** Great teacher leaders develop their knowledge of research and read external research. Along with a diverse range of data, they use research and other forms of inquiry to identify issues, inform changes, improve practice and evaluate progress. They also support colleagues in using data and research, blending this with their own knowledge to enhance their practice.

- **Facilitate sustained professional learning.** Great teacher leaders are excellent practitioners, supporting and coaching colleagues to develop great practice. Colleagues are encouraged to try things out. Learning opportunities and experiences are ongoing as part of everyday practice and occur within the learning community's culture of collaboration.

- **Are critical friends.** Great teacher leaders are constructive critics, offering challenging but supportive feedback that stimulates deep reflection. Powerful and focused questions are an important part of their repertoire in a climate where challenge among colleagues is welcomed and shapes the direction of change.

- **Build trust.** Great teacher leaders are emotionally intelligent, paying serious attention to developing relationships and giving people ownership of change processes. Time is invested in understanding colleagues' strengths and areas for development. Within a culture of positivity, they create space, listen and show empathy. Colleagues feel valued.[1]

Catalyst also highlights how teacher leaders track impact and share knowledge within and between schools.

---

[1] From L. Stoll, C. Taylor, K. Spence-Thomas and C. Brown, *Catalyst: An Evidence-Informed Collaborative, Professional Learning Resource for Teacher Leaders and Other Leaders Working in and Across Schools* (Carmarthen: Crown House Publishing, 2021).

Resource from *Creative Thinking in Schools* © Bill Lucas, Ellen Spencer, Louise Stoll, Di Fisher-Naylor, Nia Richards, Sian James and Katy Milne

Resource 16
The What and Who of Leadership

The 'what' of leadership

Other leadership issues | Leadership for creativity

The 'who' of leadership

Catalysts

School leaders

Resource from *Creative Thinking in Schools* © Bill Lucas, Ellen Spencer, Louise Stoll, Di Fisher-Naylor, Nia Richards, Sian James and Katy Milne

Resource 17
Images for Identifying, Growing and Enabling Change Catalysts

Resource from *Creative Thinking in Schools* © Bill Lucas, Ellen Spencer, Louise Stoll, Di Fisher-Naylor, Nia Richards, Sian James and Katy Milne

140 | Resources

Resource 18
What Are You Doing? What Might You Do?

	What are you already doing to …?	What (else) might you do to …?
Develop creative change catalysts with the characteristics you've identified.		
Enable and support creative change catalysts to work in your school and across other schools.		

Resource from *Creative Thinking in Schools* © Bill Lucas, Ellen Spencer, Louise Stoll, Di Fisher-Naylor, Nia Richards, Sian James and Katy Milne

Resource 19
Evidence Sheet

This photograph shows:

It shows how this school values:

Connects to this creative habit:

Because:

Resource from *Creative Thinking in Schools* © Bill Lucas, Ellen Spencer, Louise Stoll, Di Fisher-Naylor, Nia Richards, Sian James and Katy Milne

Resource 20
The Power of Language

Successful communities frequently share vocabularies. Having words for important concepts enables community members to talk about them, think together and agree on their meaning, interrogate them for deeper understanding, and gain collective clarity around related action and impact.

Language shapes thought and affects how people respond. The way we think influences the way we speak and the other way around. Changing how people talk actually changes how they think. For example, if you teach people new colour words, this changes their ability to discriminate colours.[1]

Leaders set the tone through the language they use. Language conveys what is important. It's also critical to workplace motivation. How people function at work is influenced by what and how leaders communicate. So, the language leaders use really matters; both what they say and how they say it have consequences. It's always a choice to use one word rather than another, even if it has become habitual.

The trouble with always sticking with the same terms is that language evolves over time, with experience and in context. Think about the term 'soft skills'. Creative thinking is frequently described by employers as a soft skill, but is it 'soft'? Increasingly, policymakers internationally include it within frameworks of 'capabilities' or 'competences'.

In *Teaching Creative Thinking*, Bill Lucas and Ellen Spencer instead use Art Costa and Bena Kallick's language of 'habits of mind' – 'broad, enduring and essential, lifespan learnings' – in describing five creative habits based on the Centre for Real-World Learning's five creative habits model of creative thinking.[2] As you'll also know, using the term 'playbook' to describe this leadership resource, rather than 'toolkit' or 'materials', is also a deliberate decision.

Finally, let's have a word about talk. Robert Kegan and Lisa Laskow Lahey describe workplaces as language communities.[3] Debate and discussion are very common in education language communities. Debate focuses on getting your own point across and winning an argument. Discussion avoids issues lying below the surface and blocking true and honest communication. People fiercely defend deeply held assumptions when challenged. It's easy to misunderstand others – both what they say and their intent. This leads to poor interpersonal communication which ultimately affects relationships.[4]

Getting the nature of talk right is essential. Dialogue goes beyond any individual's understanding, as team members 'suspend assumptions and enter into a genuine "thinking together" … allowing the group to discover insights not attainable individually'.[5] Dialogue helps to build sustainable community relationships in which deeper and challenging learning conversations can occur, and these are needed to develop a shared understanding of and commitment to creative thinking.

Changing language is by no means easy. It takes determined effort to use certain words and expressions rather than others. It may well necessitate changing ingrained habits, challenging others in how they use language and, of course, challenging yourself. Language has to have a meaning for the people using it, and meaning needs to be shared throughout an organisation or system to generate power and sustainability. It has to be owned and to feel that it belongs. It's about new learning for everyone which, unsurprisingly, can be really hard, but it starts with you.[6]

---

1 L. Boroditsky, How Language Shapes Thought. *Scientific American*, 304(2) (2011): 62–65.
2 B. Lucas and E. Spencer, *Teaching Creative Thinking: Developing Learners Who Generate Ideas and Can Think Critically* (Carmarthen: Crown House Publishing, 2017); A. L. Costa and B. Kallick, Preface. In A. L. Costa and B. Kallick (eds), *Learning and Leading with Habits of Mind: 16 Essential Characteristics for Success* (Alexandria, VA: Association for Supervision and Curriculum Development, 2008), pp. xvi–xxv at p. xvii.
3 R. Kegan and L. L. Lahey, *How the Way We Talk Can Change the Way We Work: Seven Languages for Transformation* (San Francisco, CA: Wiley, 2001).
4 P. Osborn and E. Canfor-Dumas, *The Talking Revolution: How Creative Conversation Can Change the World* (Oxford: Port Meadow Press, 2018).
5 P. M. Senge, *The Fifth Discipline: The Art and Practice of The Learning Organization* (New York: Doubleday, 1990), p. 10.
6 This short reading has been developed from a paper by Louise Stoll: *Language for Learning Leadership*. Occasional Paper 167 (Melbourne, VIC: Centre for Strategic Education, 2020). Available at: https://discovery.ucl.ac.uk/id/eprint/10109744.

Resource from *Creative Thinking in Schools* © Bill Lucas, Ellen Spencer, Louise Stoll, Di Fisher-Naylor, Nia Richards, Sian James and Katy Milne

Resource 21
Five Myths About Creativity

As well as being clear about what creativity is, school leaders need to be aware of a number of unhelpful myths that it may be helpful to counter if progress is to be made. The following are five of the most common myths:

1. **Creativity is too vague to be teachable.** While educational jargon such as '21st century skills' may not have helped to dispel this myth, in the last decade in England, organisations from the Confederation for British Industry to the Department for Education have used the word 'creativity' without feeling the need to explain or define it.[1]

2. **Creativity is inherited and not learned.** While genetics have a part to play in any aspect of human intelligence, in the last decade there has been growing evidence as to the teachability of creativity and the mechanisms by which it's learned.

3. **Creativity is uniquely the preserve of the arts.** In fact, while the arts do have a particular contribution to make,[2] creativity is possible in all areas of human activity, and the Durham Commission on Creativity and Education rebuts such thinking strongly.[3]

4. **Creativity detracts from the standards agenda.** Far from detracting from a proper focus on raising standards, recent research suggests that creativity might in fact contribute to raising achievement.[4]

5. **Creativity isn't connected to 'domain knowledge'.** Increasingly, it's clear from research that there are strong relationships between knowledge and creativity: Tim Atkinson emphasises the importance of domain knowledge for creativity.[5] Creativity doesn't exist in a vacuum; it's applied in a domain or context.

---

1   Confederation of British Industry, *First Steps: A New Approach for Our Schools* (London: CBI, 2012); D. Hinds, *Five Foundations to Build Character* (London: Church of England Foundation for Educational Leadership, 2019).
2   R. Alexander, The Arts in Schools: Making the Case, Heeding the Evidence. Paper presented at Curious Minds in conjunction with RECAP Conference on Intercultural Dimensions of Cultural Education, University of Chester, 13 July 2017. Available at: http://robinalexander.org.uk/wp-content/uploads/2019/12/Alexander_Curious_Minds_July17.pdf.
3   Arts Council England and Durham University, *Durham Commission on Creativity and Education* (London: Arts Council England, 2012), pp. 66–67. Available at: https://www.dur.ac.uk/resources/creativitycommission/DurhamReport.pdf.
4   D. Davies, D. Jindal-Snape, C. Collier, A. Howe, R. Digby and P. Hay, The Roles and Development Needs of Teachers to Promote Creativity: A Systematic Review of Literature. *Teaching and Teacher Education*, 41 (2014): 34–41.
5   T. Atkinson, Using the Creative Cognition Approach in Essay Assignments in Leadership Education. *Journal of Leadership Education*, 17(1) (2018): 152–161.

Resource from *Creative Thinking in Schools* © Bill Lucas, Ellen Spencer, Louise Stoll, Di Fisher-Naylor, Nia Richards, Sian James and Katy Milne

Resource 22
Thinking About Your Locality

We suggest that this table is copied out on to a flip chart sheet so that everyone in the group can add their ideas to it.[1]

However, replace the generic labels with points of interest, people, organisations and so on in your locality.

Built environment	What are you already doing well?	The natural environment
Castles and historic houses Farms and botanic gardens Monuments and parks Industrial and commercial buildings Schools Canals, railways and roads Places of worship		Seashore and coastline Fields, trees and woods Marshes, bogs and rivers Hills, peaks and mountains Dales and valleys

The locality

Social and cultural	What opportunities could be developed further?	People
Environment groups and societies Art exhibitions and galleries Libraries, museums and archives Festivals, customs and folklore		Shopkeepers Curators, archaeologists and historians Field officers Ministers Librarians and archivists Charity workers Councillors Emergency service personnel

---

1 Adapted from B. Lucas and E. Spencer, *Zest for Learning: Developing Curious Learners Who Relish Real-World Challenges* (Carmarthen: Crown House Publishing, 2020).

Resource from *Creative Thinking in Schools* © Bill Lucas, Ellen Spencer, Louise Stoll, Di Fisher-Naylor, Nia Richards, Sian James and Katy Milne

Resource 23
Signature Pedagogies for Creative Thinking

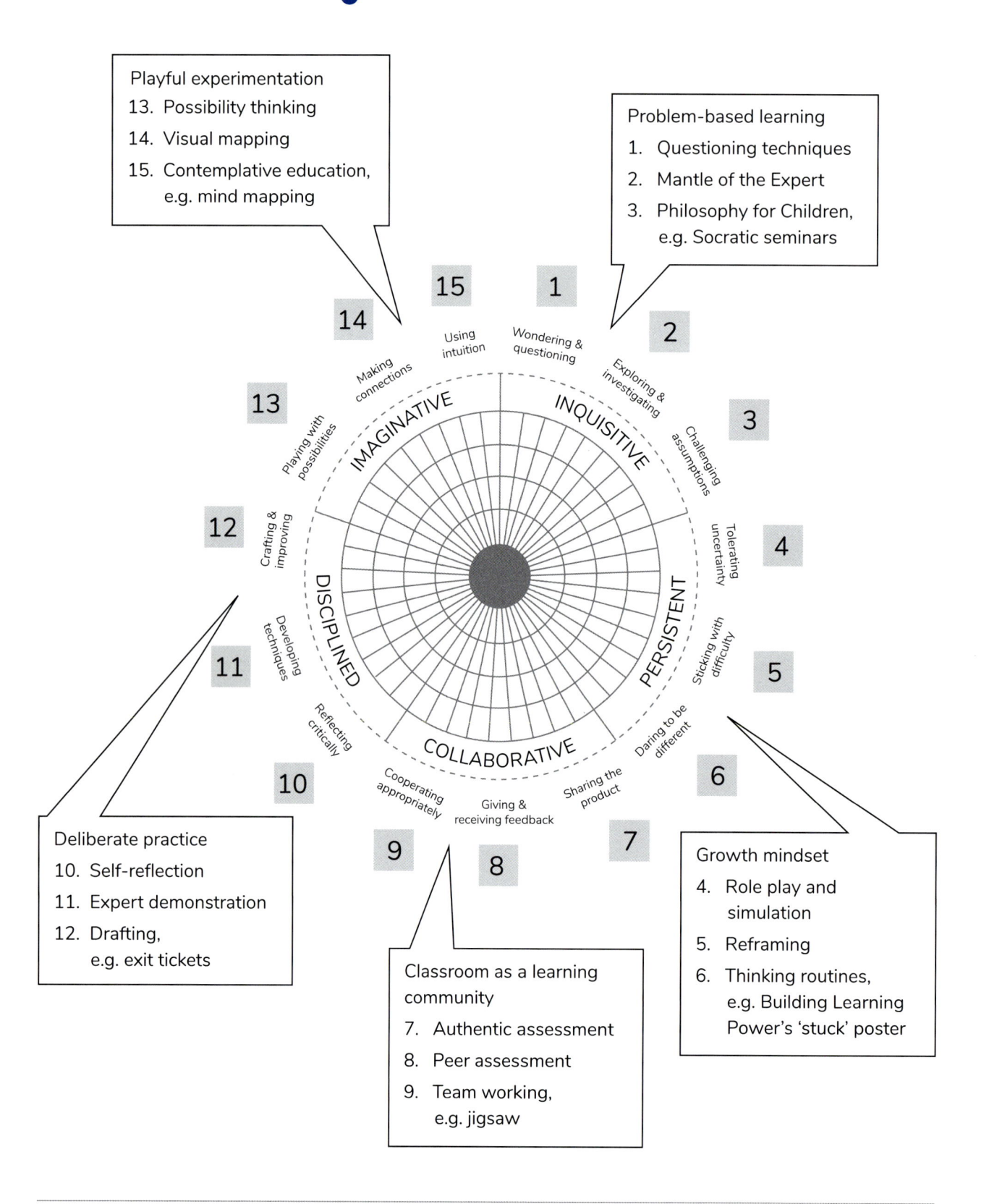

Playful experimentation
13. Possibility thinking
14. Visual mapping
15. Contemplative education, e.g. mind mapping

Problem-based learning
1. Questioning techniques
2. Mantle of the Expert
3. Philosophy for Children, e.g. Socratic seminars

Wheel segments (clockwise from top):
- IMAGINATIVE: Using intuition, Making connections, Playing with possibilities, Crafting & improving
- INQUISITIVE: Wondering & questioning, Exploring & investigating, Challenging assumptions
- PERSISTENT: Tolerating uncertainty, Sticking with difficulty, Daring to be different
- COLLABORATIVE: Sharing the product, Giving & receiving feedback, Cooperating appropriately
- DISCIPLINED: Reflecting critically, Developing techniques

Deliberate practice
10. Self-reflection
11. Expert demonstration
12. Drafting, e.g. exit tickets

Classroom as a learning community
7. Authentic assessment
8. Peer assessment
9. Team working, e.g. jigsaw

Growth mindset
4. Role play and simulation
5. Reframing
6. Thinking routines, e.g. Building Learning Power's 'stuck' poster

---

Resource from *Creative Thinking in Schools* © Bill Lucas, Ellen Spencer, Louise Stoll, Di Fisher-Naylor, Nia Richards, Sian James and Katy Milne

Resource 24
Rethinking Assessment Figures

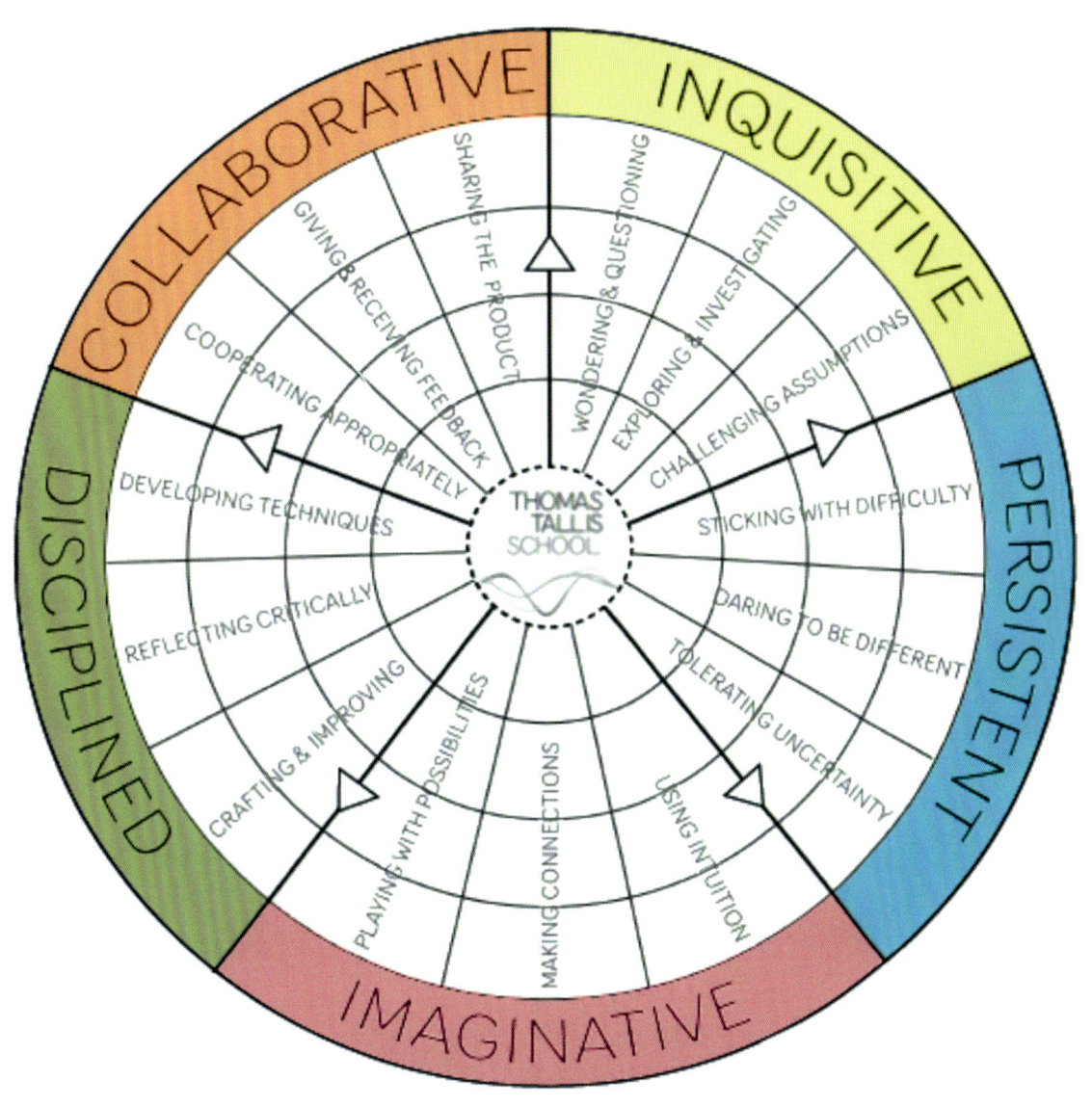

How to use the assessment wheel

Shade the segment of the circle that best represents how confident you feel about possessing each habit of mind. The levels of confidence grow in strength outwards from the centre of the wheel.

For example, as far as being imaginative is concerned, you may feel like your ability to use your intuition is just beginning whereas you're more confident in playing with possibilities. Be honest, reflect carefully and try to think of specific examples of each ability before you identify your level of confidence.

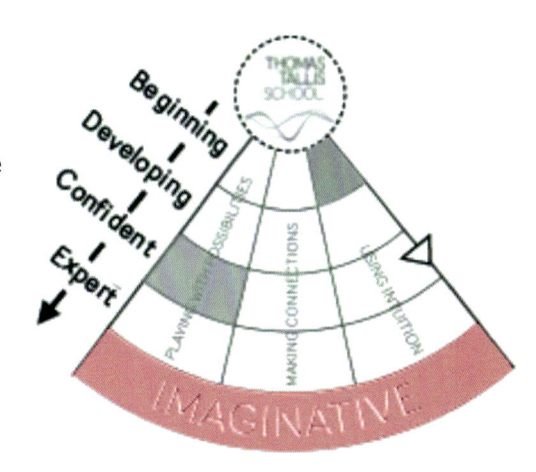

Resource from *Creative Thinking in Schools* © Bill Lucas, Ellen Spencer, Louise Stoll, Di Fisher-Naylor, Nia Richards, Sian James and Katy Milne

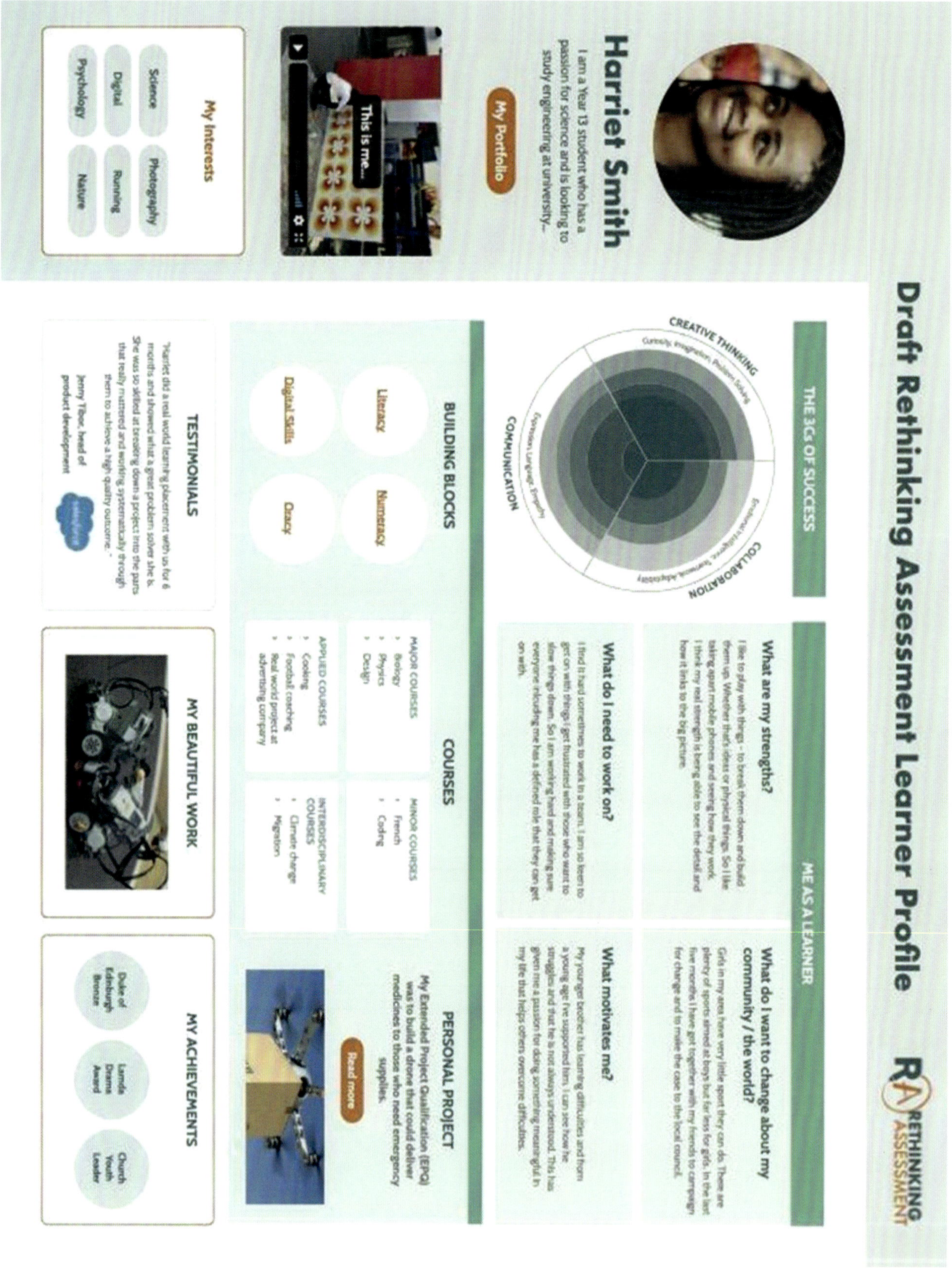

Draft Rethinking Assessment Learner Profile

Harriet Smith

I am a Year 13 student who has a passion for science and is looking to study engineering at university.

My Portfolio

This is me...

My Interests
- Science
- Photography
- Digital
- Running
- Psychology
- Nature

THE 3Cs OF SUCCESS

CREATIVE THINKING — Curiosity, Imagination, Problem Solving
COMMUNICATION — Expression, Language, Empathy
COLLABORATION — Emotional Intelligence, Teamwork, Advocacy

ME AS A LEARNER

What are my strengths?
I like to play with things – to break them down and build them up. Whether that's ideas or physical things. So I like taking apart mobile phones and seeing how they work. I think my real strength is being able to see the detail and how it links to the big picture.

What do I need to work on?
I find it hard sometimes to work in a team. I am so keen to get on with things I get frustrated with those who want to slow things down. So I am working hard and making sure everyone including me has a defined role that they can get on with.

What do I want to change about my community / the world?
Girls in my area have very little sport they can do. There are plenty of sports aimed at boys but far less for girls. In the last few months I have got together with my friends to campaign for change and to make the case to the local council.

What motivates me?
My younger brother has learning difficulties and from a young age I've supported him. I can see how he struggles and that he is not always understood. This has given me a passion for doing something meaningful in my life that helps others overcome difficulties.

BUILDING BLOCKS
- Literacy
- Numeracy
- Digital Skills
- Oracy

COURSES

MAJOR COURSES
- Biology
- Physics
- Design

MINOR COURSES
- French
- Coding

APPLIED COURSES
- Cooking
- Football coaching
- Real world project at advertising company

INTERDISCIPLINARY COURSES
- Climate change
- Migration

PERSONAL PROJECT

My Extended Project Qualification (EPQ) was to build a drone that could deliver medicines to those who need emergency supplies.

Read more

TESTIMONIALS

"Harriet did a real world learning placement with us for 6 months and showed what a great problem solver she is. She was so skilled at breaking down a project into the parts that really mattered and working systematically through them to achieve a high quality outcome."

Jenny Tibor, head of product development

MY BEAUTIFUL WORK

MY ACHIEVEMENTS
- Duke of Edinburgh Bronze
- Lamda Drama Award
- Church Youth Leader

RA — RETHINKING ASSESSMENT

Resource from *Creative Thinking in Schools* © Bill Lucas, Ellen Spencer, Louise Stoll, Di Fisher-Naylor, Nia Richards, Sian James and Katy Milne

Resource 25
A Repertoire of Methods for Assessing Creative Thinking

Pupil	Teacher	Real world	Online
Real-time feedback	Criterion-referenced grading	Expert reviews	Reliable, validated online tests
Photos	Rating of products and processes	Gallery critique	Digital badges
Self-report questionnaires	Structured interviews	Authentic tests, e.g. • Displays • Presentations • Interviews • Podcasts • Films	E-portfolios
Logs/diaries/journals	Performance tasks	Exhibitions	
Peer review	Capstone projects		
Group critique			
Badges			
Portfolios			

Resource from *Creative Thinking in Schools* © Bill Lucas, Ellen Spencer, Louise Stoll, Di Fisher-Naylor, Nia Richards, Sian James and Katy Milne

Resource 26
Learning Progression for 'Inquisitive'

Inquisitive	Starting out	Developing	Deepening	Expert
1. Posing questions	Learners use a very narrow range of questions focusing mainly on basic understanding.	Learners use a growing range of questions to suit circumstances and go beyond basic understanding.	Learners use a range of questions to suit circumstances, increasingly being able to explore, challenge and consider possibilities beyond the relatively obvious.	Learners use a wide range of questions to suit circumstances and intentions, and are able to clarify, probe, explore, infer, deduce, challenge and consider hypothetical situations.
2. Exploring and investigating	Learners view the task through a single perspective without consideration of what task elements can be changed.	Learners mainly view the task through a single perspective with little consideration of what task elements can be changed or which alternative perspectives or pathways can be considered.	Learners can shift perspective, thinking about the task/problem in a different way, considering the task/problem from a range of perspectives and are willing to test out alternative pathways.	Learners are able to see more than one side of an argument, experimenting beyond conventional perspectives, questioning the boundaries of the task to navigate around possible constraints and testing out multiple pathways, even those that seem unlikely.
3. Challenging assumptions	Learners' explorations of the task elements are very limited and they don't challenge others' opinions.	Learners' explorations are mainly routine, limited to obvious elements of the task and revisit the same ideas rather than generating new ones, only occasionally challenging others' views.	Learners demonstrate some evidence of experimentation, developing some of the task elements or synthesising existing ideas, and are increasingly able to avoid jumping to conclusions and offer opinions that differ from others'.	Learners think flexibly to develop elements of the task, effectively combining elements of a task to allow new possibilities, noticing the unusual, avoiding jumping to conclusions, recognising others' feelings and clearly articulating their own ideas.

Resource from Creative Thinking in Schools © Bill Lucas, Ellen Spencer, Louise Stoll, Di Fisher-Naylor, Nia Richards, Sian James and Katy Milne

Resource 27
Pupil Self-Report for 'Inquisitive'

Pupil name						Date	
Habit: Inquisitive							
		Not at all like me	A little like me	Quite a bit like me	Very much like me
1	I am not afraid to challenge other people's thinking.	☐	☐	☐	☐
2	I enjoy exploring things I have not learned before.	☐	☐	☐	☐
3	When I am learning something new, I can normally come up with good questions.	☐	☐	☐	☐

Resource from *Creative Thinking in Schools* © Bill Lucas, Ellen Spencer, Louise Stoll, Di Fisher-Naylor, Nia Richards, Sian James and Katy Milne

Resource 28
Twenty Professional Learning Activity Cards

Coaching or peer coaching	Lesson study
Peer observation and feedback	Reflective learning conversations

Resource from *Creative Thinking in Schools* © Bill Lucas, Ellen Spencer, Louise Stoll, Di Fisher-Naylor, Nia Richards, Sian James and Katy Milne

Learning visits, learning reviews or peer reviews

Collaborative inquiry, starting by interviewing pupils to determine their needs and focus professional learning

Subject content workshops

Induction activities and mentoring for early career teachers

Resource 28 **Twenty Professional Learning Activity Cards** | 153

Analysing and using evidence	Master's degrees/school-based master's degrees
Reading activities, e.g. book club	Action research

Writing activities/ keeping diaries or blogs	Senior leadership support for professional learning
Professional learning conversations that challenge teachers' thinking and conceptions about pupil learning	Evaluating the impact of professional learning

Resource from *Creative Thinking in Schools* © Bill Lucas, Ellen Spencer, Louise Stoll, Di Fisher-Naylor, Nia Richards, Sian James and Katy Milne

Web-based materials, videos, resources, toolkits, playbooks	
Collaborative curriculum and lesson planning	External courses

Resource 29
Powerful Professional Learning Grid

Name of activity (on card)	What are some concrete examples of this in your school(s)?	What did you/your colleagues gain from engaging in these experiences (including benefits for pupils)?	What difficulties were experienced and how were they resolved/are they being resolved?	What does this tell you about how you might use this form of professional learning to promote teaching for creativity and creative habits of mind?	What additions or adaptations might enhance its power for promoting creativity and creative thinking in teachers?

Resource from *Creative Thinking in Schools* © Bill Lucas, Ellen Spencer, Louise Stoll, Di Fisher-Naylor, Nia Richards, Sian James and Katy Milne

Resource 30
Peer Learning Prompt Cards

Ron Beghetto suggests that school and community partnerships are a form of creative learning, and through such endeavours pupils can identify complex challenges within their communities and begin to develop their own solutions – leading to valuable and long-lasting impact.[1]	According to Business in the Community, after involvement in a long-term strategic school-business partnership, '82% of schools believe that staff and students are better equipped for the future'. Furthermore, '72% of businesses report increased staff engagement, opportunities for skills development and improved internal networks'. In addition, '80% of students report their confidence or aspirations were boosted'.[2]
Drawing on international literature, Lynne Rogers and Susan McGrath found that 'a growing body of evidence has suggested that the more interactions a young person has with members of their local community, the better.'[3] In addition, offering opportunities for real-world learning not only allows teachers to work more expansively across curriculum areas, but it also impacts on pupils through increased attainment and skills development as well as motivation.	Andreas Schleicher, director of the OECD's Directorate for Education and Skills, argues that schools need to develop pupils who can think independently and are aware that there are multiple, and sometimes conflicting, perspectives: 'At work, at home and in the community, people will need a broad understanding of how others live, in different cultures and traditions, and how others think, whether as scientists or as artists.'[4]

---

1 R. A. Beghetto, *Creative Learning in Education*. In M. L. Kern and M. L. Wehmeyer (eds), *The Palgrave Handbook of Positive Education* (Cham: Palgrave Macmillan, 2021), pp. 473–491.
2 Business in the Community, *Education Toolkit: Playing Fair. Guidance for Schools and Businesses Collaborating on Curriculum-Based Projects* (2019), p. 4. Available at: https://www.bitc.org.uk/wp-content/uploads/2019/10/bitc-education-toolkit-playingfairguidanceschoolsbusinessescollaboratingcurriculumprojects-may2019.pdf.
3 L. Rogers and S. McGrath, *Edge Future Learning: Our Evidence Base* (London: The Edge Foundation, 2021), p. 33. Available at: https://www.edge.co.uk/documents/155/Edge_Future_Learning__Our_Evidence_Base.pdf.
4 A. Schleicher, Are Students Ready to Thrive in an Interconnected World? The First PISA Assessment of Global Competence Provides Some Answers. *OECD Education and Skills Today* (22 October 2020). Available at: https://oecdedutoday.com/students-ready-thrive-interconnected-world-first-pisa-assessment-global-competence.

Resource from *Creative Thinking in Schools* © Bill Lucas, Ellen Spencer, Louise Stoll, Di Fisher-Naylor, Nia Richards, Sian James and Katy Milne

Resource 31
The Peer Learning Cycle

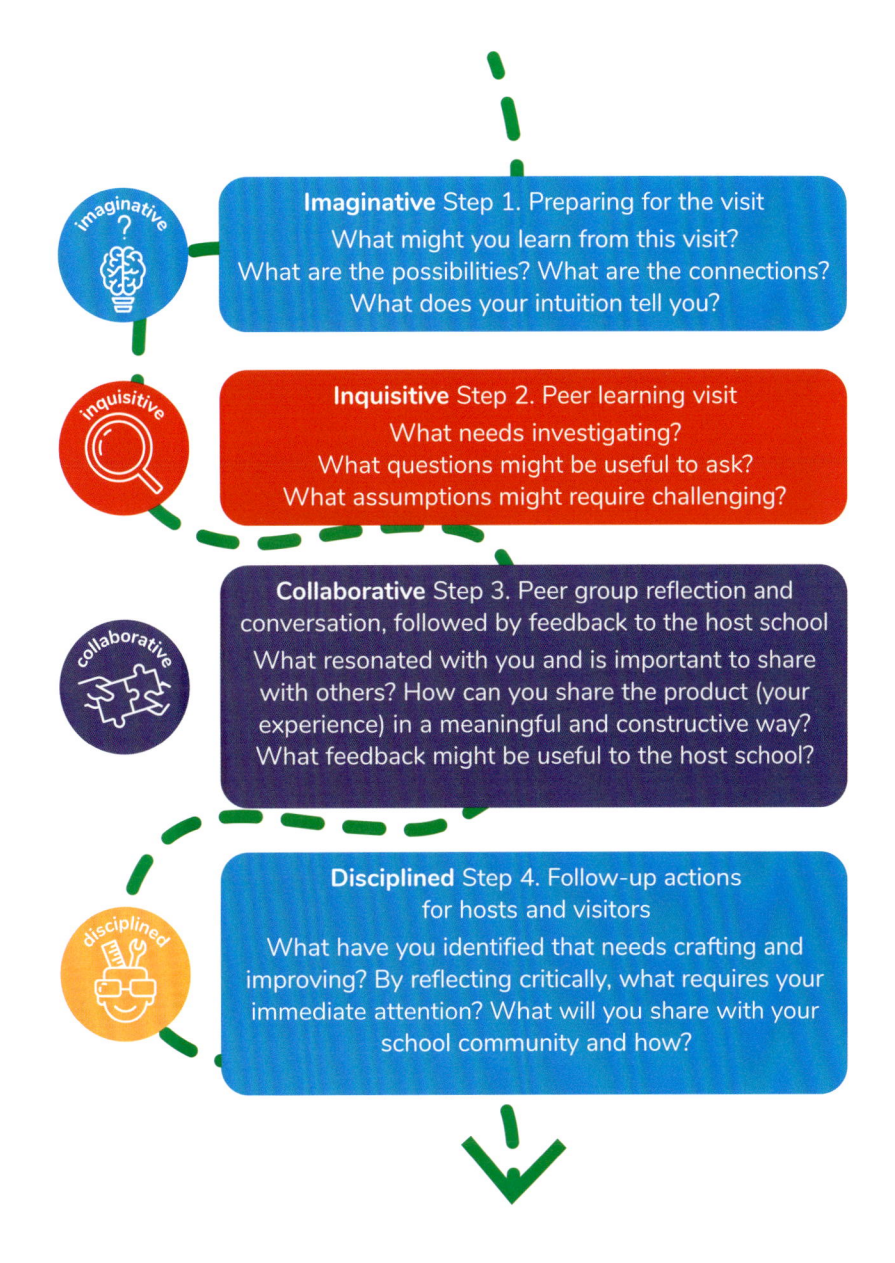

Imaginative Step 1. Preparing for the visit

What might you learn from this visit?
What are the possibilities? What are the connections?
What does your intuition tell you?

Inquisitive Step 2. Peer learning visit

What needs investigating?
What questions might be useful to ask?
What assumptions might require challenging?

Collaborative Step 3. Peer group reflection and conversation, followed by feedback to the host school

What resonated with you and is important to share with others? How can you share the product (your experience) in a meaningful and constructive way? What feedback might be useful to the host school?

Disciplined Step 4. Follow-up actions for hosts and visitors

What have you identified that needs crafting and improving? By reflecting critically, what requires your immediate attention? What will you share with your school community and how?

Resource from *Creative Thinking in Schools* © Bill Lucas, Ellen Spencer, Louise Stoll, Di Fisher-Naylor, Nia Richards, Sian James and Katy Milne

Resource 32
Richards and Hadaway Reading

In a paper published in 2020, Richards and Hadaway interviewed teachers who had been working alongside creative practitioners, such as artists, musicians and technology specialists, in the classroom over the course of a term. The researchers referred to them as hybrid teachers as they had adopted characteristics of the creative practitioner.[1]

What characteristics might a hybrid creative practitioner teacher possess, and in what ways could these characteristics benefit a teacher's practice?

---

1 Richards and Hadaway, Inter-Professionalism Between Teachers and Creative Practitioners.

Resource from *Creative Thinking in Schools* © Bill Lucas, Ellen Spencer, Louise Stoll, Di Fisher-Naylor, Nia Richards, Sian James and Katy Milne

Bibliography

Alexander, R. (2017). The Arts in Schools: Making the Case, Heeding the Evidence. Paper presented at Curious Minds in conjunction with RECAP Conference on Intercultural Dimensions of Cultural Education, University of Chester, 13 July. Available at: http://robinalexander.org.uk/wp-content/uploads/2019/12/Alexander_Curious_Minds_July17.pdf.

American Heritage Dictionaries (2011). *American Heritage Dictionary of the English Language*, 5th edn. Boston, MA: Houghton Mifflin Harcourt.

Arts Council England and Durham University (2012). *Durham Commission on Creativity and Education*. London: Arts Council England. Available at: https://www.artscouncil.org.uk/sites/default/files/download-file/Durham_Commission_on_Creativity_04112019_0.pdf

Atkinson, T. (2018). Using the Creative Cognition Approach in Essay Assignments in Leadership Education. *Journal of Leadership Education*, 17(1): 152–161.

Beghetto, R. A. (2021). *Creative Learning in Education*. In M. L. Kern and M. L. Wehmeyer (eds), *The Palgrave Handbook of Positive Education*. Cham: Palgrave Macmillan, pp. 473–491.

Boroditsky, L. (2011). How Language Shapes Thought. *Scientific American*, 304(2): 62–65.

Burner, T. (2018). Why is Educational Change So Difficult and How Can We Make It More Effective? *Forskning og forandring*, 1(1): 122–134. https://doi.org/10.23865/fof.v1.1081

Business in the Community (2019). *Education Toolkit: Playing Fair. Guidance for Schools and Businesses Collaborating on Curriculum-Based Projects*. Available at: https://www.bitc.org.uk/wp-content/uploads/2019/10/bitc-education-toolkit-playingfairguidanceschoolsbusinessescollaboratingcurriculumprojects-may2019.pdf.

Care, E., Anderson, K. and Kim, H. (2016). *Visualizing the Breadth of Skills Movement Across Education Systems*. Washington, DC: Brookings Institution. Available at: https://www.brookings.edu/research/visualizing-the-breadth-of-skills-movement-across-education-systems.

Christakis, N. (2014). The Hidden Influence of Social Networks [video]. *TED*. (14 March). Available at: https://www.ted.com/talks/nicholas_christakis_the_hidden_influence_of_social_networks?language=en.

Confederation of British Industry (2012). *First Steps: A New Approach for Our Schools*. London: CBI.

Confederation of British Industry (2019). *Educating for the Modern World: CBI/Pearson Education and Skills Survey report 2019*. London: CBI.

Combley, R. (ed.) (2011). *Cambridge Business English Dictionary*. Cambridge: Cambridge University Press.

Costa, A. and Kallick, B. (2008). Preface. In A. L. Costa and B. Kallick (eds), *Learning and Leading with Habits of Mind: 16 Essential Characteristics for Success*. Alexandria, VA: Association for Supervision and Curriculum Development, pp. xvi–xxv.

Craft, A. (2001). Little c Creativity. In A. Craft, B. Jeffrey and M. Liebling (eds), *Creativity in Education*. London: Continuum, pp. 45–61.

Cross, R., Borgatti, S. P. and Parker, A. (2002). Making Invisible Work Visible: Using Social Network Analysis to Support Strategic Collaboration. *California Management Review*, 44(2): 25–46.

Csikszentmihalyi, M. (1996). *Creativity: Flow and the Psychology of Discovery and Invention*. New York: HarperCollins.

Daly, A. J. (2010). *Social Network Theory and Educational Change*. Cambridge, MA: Harvard Education Press.

Davies, D., Jindal-Snape, D., Collier, C., Howe, A., Digby, R. and Hay, P. (2014). The Roles and Development Needs of Teachers to Promote Creativity: A Systematic Review of Literature. *Teaching and Teacher Education*, 41: 34–41.

Department for Education (2019). *State of the Nation 2019: Children's and Young People's Wellbeing*. Research Report (October). Ref: DfE-00203-2019. Available at: https://www.gov.uk/government/publications/state-of-the-nation-2019-children-and-young-peoples-wellbeing.

Gratton, L. (2022). *Redesigning Work: How to Transform Your Organization & Make Hybrid Work for Everyone*. London: Penguin Random House.

Gratton, L. and Scott, A. (2016). *The 100-Year Life: Living and Working in an Age of Longevity*. London: Bloomsbury.

Guilford, J. P. (1950). Creativity. *American Psychologist*, 5(9): 444–454.

Hanson, J., Hardman, S., Luke, S., Maunders, P. and Lucas, B. (2018). *Engineering the Future: Training Today's Teachers to Develop Tomorrow's Engineers*. London: Royal Academy of Engineering.

Hinds, D. (2019). *Five Foundations to Build Character*. London: Church of England Foundation for Educational Leadership.

Kaufman, J. and Beghetto, R. (2009). Beyond Big and Little: The Four C Model of Creativity. *Review of General Psychology*, 13(1): 1–12.

Kegan, R. and Lahey, L. L. (2001). *How the Way We Talk Can Change the Way We Work: Seven Languages for Transformation*. San Francisco, CA: Wiley.

Kools, M. and Stoll, L. (2016). *What Makes a School a Learning Organisation?* OECD Education Working Papers No. 137. Paris: OECD Publishing. Available at: https://www.oecd.org/officialdocuments/publicdisplaydocumentpdf/?cote=EDU/WKP(2016)11&docLanguage=En.

Le Fevre, D., Timperley, H., Twyford, H. and Ell, F. (2020). *Leading Powerful Professional Learning: Responding to Complexity with Adaptive Expertise*. Thousand Oaks, CA: Corwin Press.

Leithwood, K., Harris, A. and D. Hopkins (2020). Seven Strong Claims About Successful School Leadership Revisited. *School Leadership & Management*, 40(1): 5–22.

Lucas, B. (2016). A Five-Dimensional Model of Creativity and its Assessment in Schools. *Applied Measurement in Education*, 29(4): 278–290.

Lucas, B. (2021). *Creative School Leadership*. Perth: FORM.

Lucas, B. (2022). *Creative Thinking in Schools Across the World: A Snapshot of Progress in 2022*. London: Global Institute of Creative Thinking.

Lucas, B. (2022). *A Field Guide to Assessing Creative Thinking in Schools*. Perth: FORM. Available at: https://drive.google.com/file/d/19WiqUOHWgODLSxDID4RnMMD0-25dJa5F/view.

Lucas, B., Claxton, G. and Spencer, E. (2013). *Progression in Student Creativity in School: First Steps Towards New Forms of Formative Assessments*. OECD Education Working Papers No. 86. Paris: OECD Publishing. Available at: https://www.oecd.org/education/ceri/5k4dp59msdwk.pdf.

Lucas, B. and Spencer, E. (2017). *Teaching Creative Thinking: Developing Learners Who Generate Ideas and Can Think Critically*. Carmarthen: Crown House Publishing.

Lucas, B. and Spencer, E. (2020). *Zest for Learning: Developing Curious Learners Who Relish Real-World Challenges*. Carmarthen: Crown House Publishing.

Lucas, B., Spencer, E. and Stoll, L. (2021). *Creative Leadership to Develop Creativity and Creative Thinking in English Schools: A Review of the Evidence*. London: The Mercers' Company. Available at: https://www.creativityexchange.org.uk/asset/223.

Marsick, V. and Watkins, K. (2003). Demonstrating the Value of an Organization's Learning Culture: The Dimensions of the Learning Organization Questionnaire. *Advances in Developing Human Resources*, 5(2): 132–151.

National Advisory Committee on Creative and Cultural Education (1999). *All Our Futures: Creativity, Culture and Education*. Report to the Secretary of State for Education and Employment, the Secretary of State for Culture, Media and Sport. London: Department for Education and Employment. Available at: https://www.creativitycultureeducation.org/publication/all-our-futures-creativity-culture-and-education.

Organisation for Economic Co-operation and Development (2016). *What Makes a School a Learning Organisation? A Guide for Policy Makers, School Leaders and Teachers*. Paris: OECD Publishing. Available at: https://www.oecd.org/education/school/school-learning-organisation.pdf.

Organisation for Economic Co-operation and Development (2018). *Developing Schools as Learning Organisations in Wales: Implementing Education Policies*. Paris: OECD Publishing. Available at: https://www.oecd-ilibrary.org/education/developing-schools-as-learning-organisations-in-wales_9789264307193-en.

Organisation for Economic Co-operation and Development (2019a). *PISA 2018 Results: What School Life Means for Students' Lives (Volume III)*. Paris: OECD Publishing. Available at: https://www.oecd-ilibrary.org/education/pisa-2018-results-volume-iii_acd78851-en.

Organisation for Economic Co-operation and Development (2019b). *PISA 2021: Creative Thinking Framework* (Third Draft). Paris: OECD. Available at: https://www.oecd.org/pisa/publications/PISA-2021-creative-thinking-framework.pdf.

Organisation for Economic Co-operation and Development (2022). *Thinking Outside the Box: The PISA 2022 Creative Thinking Assessment*. Paris: OECD Publishing. Available at: https://issuu.com/oecd.publishing/docs/thinking-outside-the-box.

Osborn, P. and Canfor-Dumas, E. (2018). *The Talking Revolution: How Creative Conversation Can Change the World*. Oxford: Port Meadow Press.

Perkins, D. (2009). *Making Learning Whole: How Seven Principles of Teaching Can Transform Education*. San Francisco, CA: Jossey-Bass.

Petrie, C. (2020). *Spotlight: Creativity*. Helsinki: HundrED.

Richards, N. and Hadaway, S. (2020). Inter-Professionalism Between Teachers and Creative Practitioners: Risk, Exploration and Professional Identity – Learning in Situ and the Impact on Practice. *Practice*, 2: 38–52.

Rogers, L. and McGrath, S. (2021). *Edge Future Learning: Our Evidence Base*. London: The Edge Foundation. Available at: https://www.edge.co.uk/documents/155/Edge_Future_Learning__Our_Evidence_Base.pdf.

Rogers, P. (2014). *Theory of Change. Methodological Briefs: Impact Evaluation 2*. Florence: UNICEF Office of Research. Available at: https://www.unicef-irc.org/publications/pdf/brief_2_theoryofchange_eng.pdf.

Schleicher, A. (2020). Are Students Ready to Thrive in an Interconnected World? The First PISA Assessment of Global Competence Provides Some Answers. *OECD Education and Skills Today* (22 October). Available at: https://oecdedutoday.com/students-ready-thrive-interconnected-world-first-pisa-assessment-global-competence.

Senge, P. M. (1990). *The Fifth Discipline: The Art and Practice of The Learning Organization.* New York: Doubleday.

Stoll, L. (2012). Stimulating Learning Conversations. *Professional Development Today*, 14(4): 6–12.

Stoll, L. (2020a). Creative Capacity for Learning: Are We There Yet? *Journal of Educational Change*, 21(3): 421–430.

Stoll, L. (2020b). *Language for Learning Leadership.* Occasional Paper 167. Melbourne, VIC: Centre for Strategic Education. Available at: https://discovery.ucl.ac.uk/id/eprint/10109744.

Stoll, L. and Sinnema, C. (2021). Realising Curriculum Change Through Schools as Learning Organisations (SLOs) in Times of Crisis and Beyond. Paper presented at the International Congress for School Effectiveness and Improvement Virtual Congress, March.

Stoll, L., Taylor, C., Spence-Thomas, K. and Brown, C. (2021). *Catalyst: An Evidence-Informed Collaborative, Professional Learning Resource for Teacher Leaders and Other Leaders Working in and Across Schools.* Carmarthen: Crown House Publishing.

Tauritz, R. (2016). A Pedagogy for Uncertain Times. In W. Lambrechts and J. Hindson (eds), *Research and Innovation in Education for Sustainable Development: Exploring Collaborative Networks, Critical Characteristics and Evaluation Practices.* Vienna: Environment and School Initiatives, pp. 90–105.

Thompson, P., Hall, C., Jones, K. and Sefton Green, J. (2012). *The Signature Pedagogies Project: Final Report.* Nottingham: University of Nottingham.

Torrance, E. (1970). *Encouraging Creativity in the Classroom.* Dubuque, IA: William C. Brown.

Torrance, E. (1974). *The Torrance Tests of Creative Thinking: Norms-Technical Manual. Research Edition. Verbal Tests, Forms A and B. Figural Tests, Forms A and B.* Princeton, NJ: Personnel Press.

Vincent-Lancrin, S., González-Sancho, C., Bouckaert, M., de Luca, F., Fernandez-Barrerra, M., Jacotin, G., Urgel, J. and Vidal, Q. (2019). *Fostering Students' Creativity and Critical Thinking: What It Means in School.* Paris: OECD Publishing.

World Economic Forum (2015). *New Vision for Education: Unlocking the Potential of Technology.* Available at: https://www3.weforum.org/docs/WEFUSA_NewVisionforEducation_Report2015.pdf.

About the authors

Professor Bill Lucas is professor of learning and director of the Centre for Real-World Learning at the University of Winchester. A prolific researcher, writer and educational thought leader, Bill is co-founder of Rethinking Assessment and chair of the Global Institute of Creative Thinking's advisory board. Bill co-chaired the PISA 2022 Creative Thinking test, co-authored the recent Durham Commission report on creativity and education, and curates the Creativity Exchange for Arts Council England. With Ellen Spencer and Louise Stoll, Bill is the co-author of many books and reports.

Dr Ellen Spencer is senior researcher at the Centre for Real-World Learning at the University of Winchester, where she has spent over a decade researching creativity and creative leadership. She has co-authored books and reports combining conceptual development with a strongly practical focus aimed at advancing practice in the classroom. She is also a researcher for Arts Council England's Creativity Collaboratives, a three-year project to test a range of innovative practices in teaching for creativity in schools.

Professor Louise Stoll is professor of professional learning at the UCL Centre for Educational Leadership, Institute of Education, and an international consultant. Her research and development activity focuses on creating capacity for learning, including creative leadership projects. She is an associate of the Centre for Real-World Learning and Creativity, Culture and Education, as academic collaborator, critical friend and learning facilitator.

Di Fisher-Naylor is the director of Creativity, Culture and Education, the UK-based international creative learning foundation. She is a specialist in programme design, implementation and quality assurance and in professional learning for school leaders, teachers and creative professionals. Di has supported creative learning programmes across the world.

Nia Richards has been supporting professional learning in creativity since 2015, first as regional lead for a national programme in Wales and currently as programme manager for Creativity, Culture and Education. She was a classroom teacher for 13 years in secondary and further education and she has a master's degree in practitioner research.

Sian James manages a national creative learning programme with the Arts Council of Wales and has supported over 700 schools and their teachers to explore innovative pedagogy and prepare for the introduction of a new expansive curriculum. Having gained her master's degree in media at Trinity College, Sian started out as a television researcher and went on to spend over a decade working in communications for the arts and heritage sector in Wales. Sian is passionate about the arts and the sector's positive engagement with education.

Katy Milne was approached directly by TED prize-winner Professor Sugata Mitra to create and develop one of the original seven School in the Cloud labs where she worked directly with over 14,000 educators internationally. Katy was previously director of arts and creativity at Greenfield Arts for 16 years where she led an arts organisation and arts centre facility and co-created creative opportunities across educational and wider community settings across North East England.